WORKING DOGS OF THE EASTERN SIERRA

Jennifer K. Crittenden

WHISTLING
RABBIT
PRESS

San Diego, California

Contact the publisher at info@whistlingrabbitpress.com.
Contact the author, Jennifer K. Crittenden, at the website mammothletters.com.

Cover design by **Victoria Davies at VC Book Cover Designs**
Interior design by **Arc Manor Book Design**

Paperback ISBN: 978-1-950835-00-3

Publisher's Cataloging-in-Publication Data
Names: Crittenden, Jennifer K., author.
Title: Working dogs of the Eastern Sierra / Jennifer K. Crittenden.
Description: Includes index. | San Diego, CA: Whistling Rabbit Press, 2019.
Identifiers: ISBN 978-1-950835-00-3
LCCN: 2019942132
Subjects: LCSH Working dogs. | Dogs. | Rescue dogs. | Rescue work. | Guide dogs. | Search dogs. | Dogs--Therapeutic use. | Herding dogs. | Hunting dogs. | Watchdogs. | Police dogs. | Human-animal relationships. | Sierra Nevada (Calif. and Nev.) | BISAC PETS / Dogs / General
Classification: LCC SF428.5 .C75 2019 | DDC 636.73—dc23

A portion of the proceeds from sales of this book will be donated to Eastside K-9, Paws 4 Healing, Guide Dogs for the Blind, Eastern Sierra Agility Group, and Mono County Sheriff Search and Rescue Team.

WHISTLING
RABBIT
PRESS
San Diego, California

Printed in the United States of America

Published by
Whistling Rabbit Press
San Diego, California
whistlingrabbitpress.com

To Jet

Contents

Trico

TRICO is an Entlebucher Mountain Dog, a rare breed in the US. "I've probably said 'Entlebucher Mountain Dog' 500 times," sighed his owner, Steve. As an avalanche dog on Mammoth Mountain, Trico gets a lot of publicity. There's even a Trico plushie, an accurate replica of him in stuffed animal form that the Mountain sells in their retail outlets. One summer day, Steve and Trico were walking down the street, Steve in flip-flops and Trico on a leash. A family pulled over in a car, and a little boy leaned out and called, "Is that Trico?" Surprised, Steve affirmed that it was, and the boy held a stuffed Trico out the window and announced, "I've got one!" The Mountain, the ski patrollers, and Eastside K-9, the nonprofit that supports the avalanche dogs, use the plushies and dogs for educational purposes, to teach about snow safety. "People listen to people with cute dogs," Steve said. Eastside K-9 founder, Sean, added, "Talking about avalanches can be scary. Having a dog there makes it more digestible."

Steve acquired Trico three years ago from a breeder in San Clemente. He drove down with a couple other patrollers to assess a litter of puppies that had been sired by a well-known agility dog. "We went to the beach and got a dog," Steve said. Eastside K-9 has developed an adaptive puppy test to help them select dogs that are likely to flourish as avalanche dogs. Each patroller independently assesses the puppies, and then they all compare notes. "It can be kind of a marginal distinction," said Steve. "We try to make it objective." Trico was the clear favorite, particularly because of his performance in the confined space test. The patrollers bring a long dark and dreary box with them and toss a toy inside to see if the puppy will go in after it. They don't want a puppy that will rush in after it willy-nilly, nor do they want one that refuses to go in at all.

Patroller Scott explained, "This is a tough one for puppies. Some dogs won't have anything to do with it. But we've got deep dark holes that the dogs are supposed to go into. We do searches at night and send them into tree wells. They have to be comfortable in tight spaces."

Trico sniffed cautiously around the box, looked at Steve, and then walked in to retrieve the toy, like the high achiever he is. He also did well in the hang test, where a patroller supports the puppy under his belly with his legs and paws hanging free. Trico didn't struggle or freak out; he just looked at Steve, like, "What's next?"

Steve is a fly fishing guide, and he named Trico after a small powerful insect used as a lure. Trico is a little shorter than the other avalanche dogs, mostly black and yellow Labs, but not the lightest, weighing 52 pounds now. When Steve got him as a puppy at eight weeks, he started training with him right away. "I put him in my jacket and took him up the chairlift," he said. "He was probably thinking, 'One day I'm looking at whales; the next day I'm on a chairlift looking at acres of snow.'" Trico got fully certified last year.

Steve started as a helper in the program eight years ago, eventually moving up to secondary handler before being voted in as a primary handler by the Eastside K-9 Board. "We all work our way through the ranks," he said. "It's a process. You have to test the waters and see how you do. It's a big commitment. A primary handler has to demonstrate maturity and have the life faculties to support the program. It should be a labor of love." Overall he is impressed with the program. "It's developed into this well-balanced, beautiful thing that works for everybody," he said.

Trico developed an occlusion in his stomach last year and was put on leave while he went through surgery. It happened that the patrollers were working

a controlled avalanche off the face of Climax after the vet had seen Trico. After using his beacon, Steve turned his phone back on in time to receive a call from the vet saying Trico was good to go. Steve immediately went down to pick him up, and a few minutes later, Trico was working the avalanche with 40 staples in his stomach, bringing the total of dogs on the scene that day to four, a record high.

Last year, there was a large avalanche in a closed area. Steve said, "We sent in the dogs to make sure no one was accidentally caught up in it. The dogs did well. They found some pieces of trash, things that weren't supposed to be there." But, fortunately, no people. Steve said, "My desire is that Trico never has to be deployed. The dogs are an insurance policy." Although Mammoth has Class A avalanche terrain, Steve attributes the Mountain's safety record to a long history of training on the human side, good avalanche control equipment, as well as a stable snow pack. "We just don't seem to have as many incidents as in Canada or the northern Rockies," he said.

The "Entles" were bred for high alpine herding, but Steve was surprised when they were around some sheep one day and Trico started herding them. Another day, he came upon an abandoned Frisbee and chucked it. Trico caught it on the first try. Steve said, "Sometimes trainers say if you have a good dog, don't mess it up. We humans can get in the way."

He thinks a lot about dog training. "I read a lot of books coming into this, but at the end most will say, 'You're going to learn your dog.' That bond is the most important thing. I believe every dog is as unique as we are, and you have to learn what you can work with. Sometimes you find a tangent, and you go with it. It's very fluid, very dynamic. You can go in with a particular mindset, an objective, and you come out with a completely different result. It's like the difference between writing a technical manual and writing poetry; things can go way down the river." Nevertheless he adds, "Why did I get into dog training? Because my 13-year-old self was giving me a high five. It's just a super cool thing."

Dante and Mulligan

"THAT dog was a piece of work," Alix said of her first agility dog. Angie was fast, but sometimes it was just an accident if she went in the right direction. "She'd check out what I was saying," Alix said, "and be like 'yeah . . . no.'" Alix started the Australian Cattle Dog in agility after her independent spirit was observed by a wise dog trainer who told Alix, "That dog needs a job." It took Angie nine years to be awarded an agility champion title, by acquiring a certain number of competitive points during North American Dog Agility Council trials.

"If you compete enough, you'll get the points," explained Alix. But, as a teacher in Bishop, she had difficulty finding much time to travel. Her current agility dog, Dante, is a sharp contrast. "He's more slow and steady," said Alix. "He wants to get it right." His hard work has paid off. He has acquired five NADAC Agility Trial Champion titles, so-called NATCHs, and he's only seven.

Agility trials are an opportunity for competitive dogs and trainers to display amazing communication skills as the trainers guide the dogs through an obstacle course, using body language, hand signals, and verbal commands. The objective is to complete the course in a prescribed order and as fast as possible. Videos of championship runs demonstrate such techniques as drawing an invisible line in front of the dog for it to follow, as well as showcasing some superb canine athletes.

Each course is unique and comprised of a variety of hurdles, such as jumps, dog walks, A-frames, hoops, barrels and weave poles. Obstacles are sometimes set right next to each other, forcing the trainer to convince the dog to choose the right one. Courses and obstacles are designed to challenge both dogs and trainers. When the NADAC added hoops to their trials, they explained with a hint of mischief (and glee), "They are a great highlight of late or bad handling. If you're late [with a command], your dog is still running full speed in the wrong direction!"

NADAC courses often require the trainer to work at a distance from the dog. "Some dogs want to be close to the trainer," Alix explained. A key trait of a serious agility dog is "drive," the desire to work. She said that Dante is of a different temperament. "He's happy just to be with me. He doesn't have as much at stake. He just likes to look good out there."

Her third dog, Mulligan, is a different story. Alix was honored to receive the Australian Shepherd from a trainer who raises champion agility dogs. "I was floored," she said. Mulligan's breeding is evident in her speed, her ability to pivot on the run, and how good she is on her feet. She's also really into it. "You can see her thinking, 'What does she want me to do?'" Alix said. Mulligan is only 11 months old and too young to compete, but Alix has started practicing with her. "She catches on fast," said Alix. "She's a hard worker. When she comes home from training, she's not just physically tired. She's brain-tired."

Will everything come together for the new Aussie? Alix has high hopes, but time will tell. "She's my Mullie," said Alix. "She's my do-over after Angie."

Tinker

TINKER may look like just a sweet yellow Lab puppy, but she is hard at work in Mammoth Lakes, learning the basics that make up the early training for a guide dog for the blind. She must learn obedience, where to walk relative to her trainer, not to jump or pick things up, not to be distracted by noises and other dogs, and to get acclimated to public places and public transportation. She must also learn to relieve herself on command on all kinds of surfaces, which is a tough hurdle.

She has just turned six months old and will stay with her puppy raiser for another eight to ten months. Then she will be evaluated back at the main campus of the Guide Dogs for the Blind in San Rafael for health and temperament. If she is one of the best of the best, she will be chosen as a breeder and placed with a nearby family. If not, she will be spayed and start the intensive 12-week training program specific to guide dogs where they learn about challenges such as overhead obstacles, hybrid cars, curbs, and potholes. They even learn intelligent disobedience, when they may disobey a command because it would put their person in danger. The highly selective dog training done by Guide Dogs for the Blind was documented in the 2018 film "Pick of the Litter."

Guide dogs serve as a mobility aid, helping a blind person to become more active and independent, as well as providing companionship. Because of the length and complexity of the training and ongoing veterinary financial assistance, it costs well over $100,000 to support a guide dog team throughout its working life together. Guide Dogs for the Blind provides their services free of charge and is entirely funded by donations.

Tinker knows none of this. She just loves her puppy raiser, Anne, and always wants to snuggle. "She's a fun little puppy. She seems pretty smart. She really likes people, which could be her downfall," Anne said. Guide dogs are not allowed to socialize when they are working. "Oh, look, she knows I'm talking about her so she's brought me a toy," she added.

This is Anne's sixth puppy. "I always say I'm going to take a break, but it never lasts and I go get a puppy," she said. The puppies are bred and born at the San Rafael campus, and all the puppies' names from the litter start with the same letter. "Each puppy is so different," said Anne. "They each present with things that are easy and things that are challenges." When she brought Tinker home, if she left her side, to go even a few feet away, Tinker would start barking her head off. "What am I going to do?" Anne asked herself. "How am I going to take a shower?" Fortunately, Tinker outgrew that in a few days.

The puppy raisers themselves undergo considerable training, usually starting off as a puppy sitter, where they take a dog for a short period of time. It can take from four to six months of dog sitting and attending meetings to become qualified as a puppy raiser. Raisers have to understand the multiple leashes, collars, and cables, deliver treats (only kibble dry dog food) directly to the dog's mouth so it doesn't grab for the food, and correctly put on a Gentle Leader®, which looks like a muzzle but is a tool to train the dog not to pull on the leash. Only certain toys are allowed (no squeak toys), and no bedding is allowed in their crate. Because the Labs chew, these rules keep the puppy safe. Puppy raisers don't expend a lot of their own funds because the club is able to provide food and Guide Dogs for the Blind pays for the veterinary care.

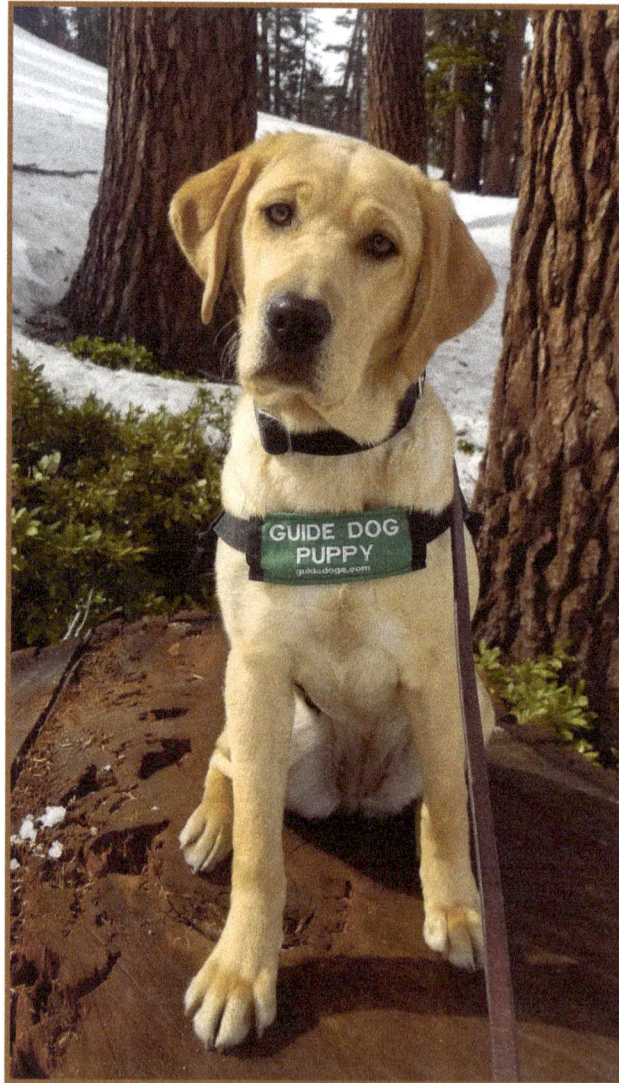

Most guide dogs are Labradors or Golden Retrievers, and the puppy raisers use the dogs' natural instincts to guide the training. "Goldens are interested in affection," said Anne, "but Labs are all about the food." Puppy raisers carry a bait bag filled with kibble whenever they have the dog on a leash, so they can reward the dog when it is behaving well. They use a training technique of positive reinforcement, so the dog learns to walk in the proper position. "They learn 'when I walk here, I get more food,'" said Anne.

"There's a big misconception that they're not allowed to be dogs," said Anne. "They're not working 24/7. But when that vest goes on, everything has to kick in." Many dogs don't pass the requirements to become a guide dog which can be a disappointment for the raiser when they have put in so much work. "You can't put a square peg in a round hole," said Anne. Dogs who don't make it may go on to have other jobs, such as search and rescue or medical alert dogs. "It all works out in the end," she said. "I feel like the dogs ended up where they were meant to be."

The local group started when a puppy raiser for the Guide Dogs for the Blind moved to Bishop, bringing her puppy with her. After driving to Ridgecrest for meetings, she started looking around for others to start a club in the Mammoth/Bishop area. They now have about six puppy raisers, and a number of potential recruits showed up at a recent Puppy 101 training session where they learned about the requirements and responsibilities. Anne explained to the attendees that teaching the dogs to relieve themselves on command is a big part of the training. "We talk a lot about poop," she warned them.

Anne used to work as a dog obedience trainer, but she got discouraged when the owners wouldn't put in the work to correctly train their dogs and were looking for a quick solution. "They'd complain that the puppy peed in the house at ten weeks, but it takes a human baby several years to be potty trained," she said. She also said there's more understanding now about learning theory in housebreaking a dog. "People are going more in the way of 'Don't smack your kids and don't hit your dog.' If your dog makes a mistake, maybe hit yourself with the newspaper because you didn't get it out soon enough," she said.

At the meeting, the puppy raisers were mourning the departure of a pup who had gone off for more training in an urban environment. The dogs have to learn to cope with buses, semis, elevators, shopping malls, all situations where their eventual owner might want to go. Club members who had grown attached to the dog got a little choked up. "Oh, yeah, there's lots of tears when the dogs leave," Anne said. "Everybody cries." On the other hand, she said, "We're really motivated to help these inspiring dogs be successful."

Bolt the Heeler

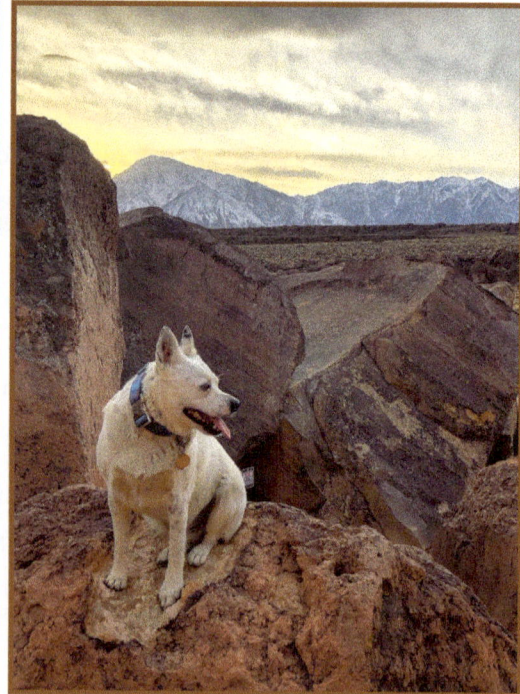

LEA and her husband noticed when the little white dog stopped showing up at their paddock. Nearly every day for months, the puppy would swim across the creek and join them as they gave riding or roping lessons in the corral. This day, no dog. They started asking around, and, sure enough, the dog had been caught dodging traffic in front of the casino and taken to the pound. "Please let us take him," Lea pleaded to the shelter staff. "He already knows us, we have other dogs, we're approved for adopting, please, please, please." And the staff said yes.

They named him Bolt after the cartoon dog, and Bolt declared himself Patroller of the Paddock. If the chickens start squabbling, he lowers his head and breaks it up. If the cats pick a fight with feral cats, he runs through the middle and busts them apart. He is also busy mentoring a new puppy named Makoons which means "bear cub" in Chippewa. If Lea dawdles on her way into the house, he'll nip at her heels, as if to say, "Get in there!" When cattle or horses need to be moved, he's on the job, striding around importantly with his tail up. If the horses paw and toss their heads, he glowers with an expression that says, "Dude! Knock it off! You're messing up!" He likes to keep things shipshape with his herd because he's in charge.

Not in the mind of the ornery pony though. If Bolt isn't watching, the pony will try to kick him. If the pony isn't looking, Bolt will take a nibble out of his leg. In the barnyard pecking order, they both think they are top dog.

Bolt is the ultimate sidekick, everybody's shadow. There's lots of action at the Bishop homestead with animals, wrestling boys, visitors, and drones. Bolt loves every minute, even howling along with the noon whistle. He's always game for rough-housing, hiking, a walk downtown, swimming in the lakes, fishing, even a turn on the trampoline. He goes nuts over a laser beam and has been known to play tug-of-war with the fence. He looks delighted when Lea rolls her eyes and thanks him for rolling in horse manure. Bolt doesn't get sarcasm. He enjoys performing tricks, like high five and playing dead when someone "shoots" him. "Sometimes it's a total circus around here," said Lea.

Like many locals, he works more than one job. His busy lifestyle is documented on an Instagram account which has over 3,000 followers, and he is well known for his rodeo adventures and his travels up and down US Highway 395. Lea sometimes draws a ring around his eye or sketches on eyebrows. He's a huge hit with the kids, and they don't mind when he licks their faces because he has an unusual smooth, soft tongue.

As is typical of Australian Cattle Dogs, sometimes called Queensland Heelers, Bolt is thick and sturdy at 55 pounds. "We call him our little tank," Lea said. The Heelers were recognized as a separate breed by the American Kennel Club for competitions as recently as 1980. Bolt himself competed at Indian Days to be named the best "Rez Dog," but he lost to some big, tough bruiser. He's still the best in his own mind.

Takoda and Ayla

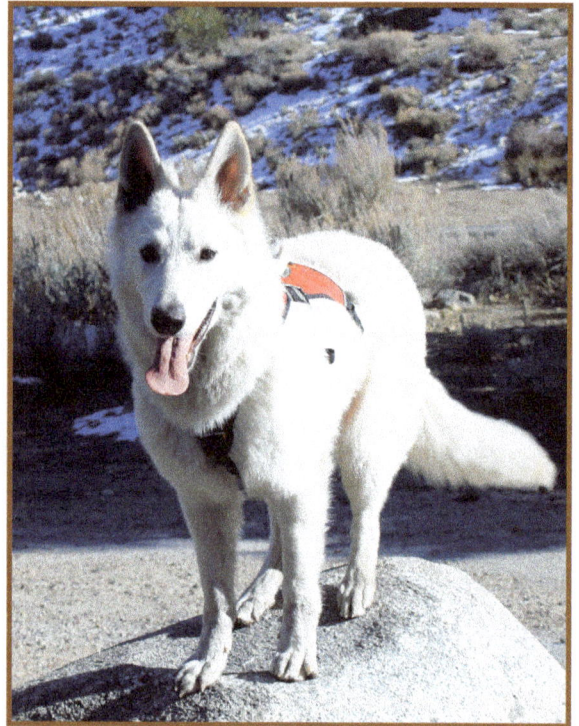

CHRISTINA got Takoda because of King, Mammoth Mountain's first avalanche dog. "He definitely affected my choice for a dog," she said. "Plus a Golden Retriever seemed like a good breed for a working dog." They started training in search and rescue when Takoda was nine months old, and he went on his first real mission at about three years old on Matterhorn Peak near Bridgeport. He was with the Mono County Sheriff Search and Rescue for five years. At that point, Christina became concerned that he was no longer at the top of his game. "Working dogs retire at about seven or eight," she said. "That's just how it goes."

She was interested in search and rescue even before she got Takoda. She moved to Mammoth Lakes after college and began to learn about alpine sports and mountaineering. In 2004, she broke her back skiing and spent six years going through surgeries. After a full recovery, it was time to help out other outdoor enthusiasts who found themselves in similar trouble. During the years of healing, she met King, and the idea of having an animal partner helping to rescue people sounded perfect. She trained with a search dog group out of Nevada until the driving got old, and eventually she hooked up with Mono County Sheriff Search and Rescue.

Training search and rescue dogs is different from training tracking dogs who work on a leash and follow a particular scent. "With an air scent dog, you're teaching them to use their nose to pick up any human smell," she said. It takes years to train a solid SAR dog, and, being a working individual herself, Christina could only train on the weekends. "You have to be so careful. It takes time," she said. "You have to protect your puppy from frightening experiences. When Takoda was in the car one time, the dog gate fell on him, and he still freaks out if you rattle a gate. You have to be really careful with the helicopter training," she added.

Most search and rescue callouts come in for people whose general location is known, such as injured hikers. The scent dogs are used when you have no idea where the person needing assistance is, which doesn't happen as often. "It's a big game to them," Christina said. "They're just working so they can play with their favorite toy." Because some of the missions ended in tragic discoveries, she was careful to reward him and celebrate their success when they were out of sight of other people.

They were once called out when someone observed some people setting off into the wilderness with almost no supplies. Takoda and Christina took off after them before they were eventually informed that the hikers were ultra-lightweight backpacking enthusiasts and were fine. "We would never have caught them," she chuckled. "But Takoda thought it was great fun."

Following in Takoda's footsteps is Ayla, a White Swiss Shepherd, who is almost two years old and is going through training. Christina became interested in the breed because many Canadian patrollers use them. After some research, she got on the waiting list of a breeder in Washington. A few years and many conversations later, the breeder ended up donating the valuable dog to the search and rescue team with Christina designated as her handler.

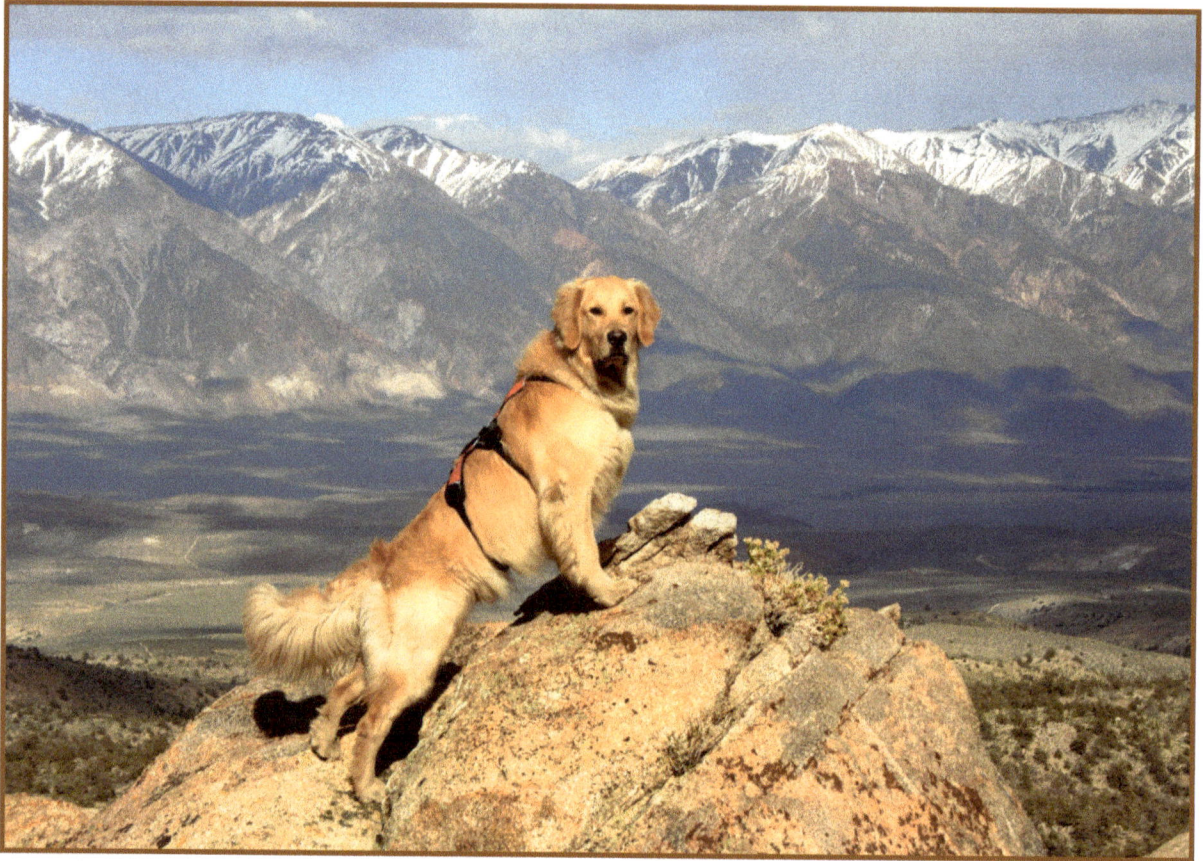

She thought the color and breed might offer some advantages over Goldens. Takoda used to get snow balls on his feet, and she wondered if the shepherd might do better in the deep Sierra snow. With her white coat, she seems better able to regulate her temperature whereas Takoda was prone to overheating. She's also much easier to spot in the woods. Christina used to put a bell on Takoda before she sent him out to follow up on a scent. "I had no idea where he was," she said. "Sometimes I'd be standing there by myself for five minutes."

Christina was also in the market for a smaller dog because Takoda weighed 85 pounds. "I couldn't believe it when one guy put him on his shoulder. I can't even lift him," she said. Ayla's mother was quite small, so Christina was hopeful the puppy wouldn't get too big. No such luck. She weighs in at 65 pounds today. Christina explained that rescue dogs have gotten smaller over the years, especially because of the need to ride in helicopters. "That's why the St. Bernards got phased out," she said.

Another big difference with Ayla is her drive. "She's very athletic and fit. She can go for eight to ten hours," Christina said. "My Golden couldn't do that." She also has a very different temperament. "Labs and retrievers are very adaptable. They are happy to work but are just as happy to lay around the house," Christina said. "Shepherds are aloof; they're really only interested in their people and have a constant drive to work or be challenged." Because of this, Ayla's stimulation requirement is much higher. "During busy work weeks when she doesn't get that much stimulation, I sometimes say 'I can't live with you right now,' and we go play fetch in the hallway," she said. Christina takes her hiking and cross-country skiing and said as long as she's exercised, she's all right to share a house with.

Christina is taking her training very slowly and backs off if she thinks the dog is getting stressed, but Ayla is making good progress. All eyes are on her because there are no other dogs in the Mono County Sheriff Search and Rescue team just now. Her future in the big game of finding people awaits.

Katie and Katie Belle

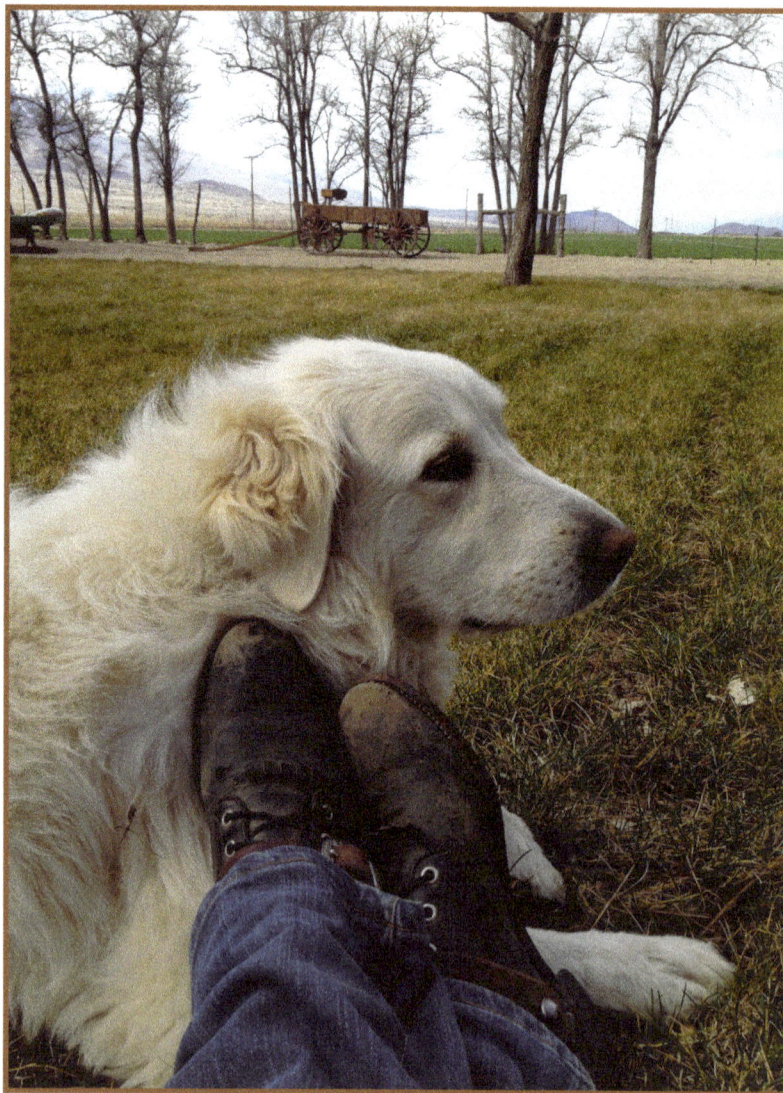

"**THAT** dog probably took five years off my life," Jennifer said about Katie. The pack station and ranch had more history with Shepherds, but once Jennifer saw the Great Pyrenees puppy, there was no way to resist. Katie was raised as a family pet. "We didn't train her," said Jennifer. "Well, she trained us."

Katie decided that since there was no herd to protect, she would designate herself the protector of the livestock, the horses and mules. She drew her boundary lines and wouldn't allow anything she didn't like inside those lines. She wouldn't tolerate coyotes, hated crows, and didn't care for pigeons much. While sheep and goats naturally take to a protector, mules usually hate dogs and can be aggressive. Katie won them over. "They would lie down with her," said Jennifer. "It was craziness. It was like she said, 'Look, I have determined this to be my purpose in life,' and finally the mules said, 'Okay, fine, you win.' She was loved."

Katie was also loved by the many people who came to the McGee Creek pack station. "She was beyond friendly," said Jennifer. "She would make a beeline for the kids. I used to wonder if a robber came, if she would have asked him to rub her belly."

But she roamed. As a puppy, she would wander from the pack station down to the campground to visit the campers. Jennifer tried to keep her in her kennel, but she hated it. "You'd think you were torturing her," she said. "I couldn't take it. I felt like a terrible person." And she would manage to escape. When Jennifer left Katie with a friend, Katie would swim underwater under a fence over a creek to escape so she could go play in the park with the kids. Down at Jennifer's ranch off US Highway 395, Katie would venture over to the fish hatchery to see what those people were up to. The breeder had warned Jennifer, "These dogs need a lot of territory," but Katie's boundaries were expanding.

One year, unbeknownst to Jennifer, Katie started going to visit a construction crew widening the roadway. While the traffic was stopped, she would go from car to car, panhandling. One afternoon, she befriended a trucker who was concerned about the big white dog in the middle of nowhere. He hoisted her into his truck and drove off. Jennifer was frantic by 6 p.m. when the dog hadn't come home. She called the shelter, and, although the shelter staff were familiar with Katie because of her independent spirit, they hadn't seen her. Jennifer drove around all night, looking for Katie. In the morning, the shelter called back. "You're looking for Katie, right?" the staff said. "Well, she's in Reno." The trucker had phoned to say that he was coming back through and could drop her off. Katie had stayed in his sleeper with him, where he fed her hamburgers on her big adventure. Jennifer had to pay the shelter $50 to get her back, and that wasn't her last trip to the shelter to pick up Katie.

Another day, Katie was checking out the back fence where a family of tourists had stopped on their way home from skiing. They were confused to see an unleashed dog and took her with them. They were in Lancaster before they realized that buried in all the fur were tags and a collar. They noted Jennifer's exchange and concluded the dog must be from Los Angeles. They drove on. They were in Capistrano before they called Jennifer. "We can drop her off," they said gaily. "What the heck?" said Jennifer. "I'm in Independence, you idiot!" She had to drive 300 miles to get Katie back that time.

18

Years after the fact, Jennifer learned that Katie had established a separate life with a family across the highway. They had set her up with her own bed and were feeding her. "You can't do that," Jennifer said on the phone. "It's too dangerous." Her intuition was right. Katie's wanderlust was ultimately her undoing when she got hit by a car.

Then came Katie Belle, another adorable Great Pyrenees puppy. Jennifer kenneled her and crated her from the get go, and Katie Belle was much more of a homebody. Following in Katie's footsteps, she befriended the horses and mules and charmed the visitors. She too patrolled her boundaries, but they were set much closer to the house. Still, when you spotted her at a distance, you might have guessed it was Katie's ghost on the horizon, before she turned to venture further.

Señor Javier

"**NOW** remember, we're just here to learn," Sonja's husband reminded her when they walked into the event featuring guide dogs for the blind. "We're not here to get a dog."

But Sonja was already smitten with the six-month-old yellow Lab sitting quietly by his trainer. Over the next year, while volunteering for the organization, both Sonja and her husband fell in love with Javier's personality and big heart. At that point, Javier got kicked out of guide dog school for having a mind of his own—half of the dogs who start the training don't graduate—and he was considering a career change. His trainer turned him over to Sonja with four conditions: she would have first dibs to dog sit when Sonja needed a sitter, Javier would continue to mentor the guide dog puppies, he would take up work as a therapy dog so that his training didn't go to waste, and he would become a 49ers fan.

The last condition nearly threw Sonja. "Is that football?" she asked, then grinned. So the team of Sonja and Señor Javier came to be, Javier sporting his therapy dog vest and a red and gold collar, San Francisco colors. They occasionally visit a senior care home and a rehabilitation center, but they try to never miss their monthly visits to a center for the handicapped.

Anywhere from 10 to 18 people gather, excited about their chance to meet with the therapy dog. They take turns walking Javier, who is now six years old. "He's just a normal dog, but as soon as he puts the vest on, he becomes a serious and well-behaved dog," Sonja said. Sometimes he gets walked up and down the hallway fifty times, but he never objects.

The effect on the disabled is remarkable. Sonja said her favorite part is to see the physical signs of enjoyment on the faces of the residents. One aide told her that she sees more smiles that day than at any other time. One time, Javier strolled over and placed his head on the knee of a woman in a wheelchair. She smiled down at him. "I've never seen her smile before," an attendant whispered to Sonja.

Sonja previously volunteered as a court advocate for a ten-year-old boy who had been abused. "He was completely closed off," said Sonja. "It was like there was a wall around him." Then he met Javier. The boy lit up, and the two rolled around in the grass and played for an hour. "He turned back into a kid. With Javier, the little guy was safe and free and childlike," said Sonja.

Javier encounters a lot of kids in his other job as a greeter at Sonja's real estate office. Parked outside her door on a long tie-down, he welcomes the passersby. "He's awesome with kids," she said. "They pull on his ears or his tail, but he just loves them." He's so popular, she jokes that he brings in business. "He's my walking billboard," she said. He even has his own Facebook page where he can meet even more people.

Therapy dogs are not considered service dogs, but they have been carefully trained to provide comfort and affection to people. They are taught to stay calm in crowded situations and tolerate loud noises and fast movements. They must always be friendly to strangers, but never jump on them, and be at ease constantly meeting new people. To become a certified therapy dog, Javier had to go through a test proving that he had the proper training, temperament, and characteristics to wear the official therapy dog vest.

Journey

SOME might think that Journey's work as a human remains recovery dog is at least sobering, if not depressing. She doesn't see it that way. To her, it's about discovery, success, solving a mystery, resolution.

For her handler, it's not that simple. Mike and his wife both work in search recovery, and they make an effort not to talk too much about that work. "I try not to think too deeply about it," he said. "But sometimes you can't help yourself."

He and Journey were called up to the Eastern Sierra to help search for Karlie Guse after the sixteen-year-old had been missing for several weeks. They were accompanied by a local, who served as flanker, someone who searches a little but mostly supports the canine unit. "Thankfully, we didn't find anything, but when someone's been missing that long, it's not a good sign," he said.

After Mono County contacted the state Office for Emergency Services for a recovery dog, the call went out to California counties with those resources. Mike and Journey are volunteers with the Riverside County Sheriff's Department and got the assignment. Over three days, they searched some canyons where mines are located near Karlie's home in Chalfant. For the mines that had a vertical shaft, Mike walked Journey on lead along the top of the shafts where the air blows out to see if her nose would go up, but they found nothing. The landscape astonished Mike. "It's a beautiful area, but you have to keep your head screwed on because you have a job to do," he said.

At seven years old, Journey has been certified every year for the last five years. The demand for recovery is greater than for live searches, so she got certified as a human remains recovery dog two and a half years ago. They have worked the Camp Fire, the Santa Barbara mudslides, and recently began working with Aguilas del Desierto with whom they search for the bodies of immigrants who have died in the desert, trying to cross the border. "I don't get into the politics of it," said Mike. "But it's been very eye-opening. People are being pushed to remote areas to cross." They recently found the remains of eight people who had died of exposure. The addition of a dog is very helpful because she can cover ground much faster than a human because of her nose. Human remains, even bones, give off a lot of scent.

They were recently involved in a search that turned into a crime scene when they discovered evidence involved in a missing person case. The GPS tracking device that Journey wears was able to pinpoint the location of items that led to a father being charged with torture and murder in the disappearance of his eight-year-old son although no body has been found. "We've been out four times to search for the boy. It's frustrating because there has been no closure in the case," said Mike.

Another case in Idyllwild also affected him emotionally. A 82-year-old man had disappeared, and the family thought he wouldn't have walked far because he was uneasy on trails. Mike and

Journey went on three missions without finding him. After several weeks, the man's Springer Spaniel appeared back in town, and Mike and Journey went back for another search. The elderly Spaniel led them up a paved road to a water tank, but then got tired or confused and stopped. A teammate found the man's body half a mile further up. The man had died of hypothermia, probably on the first night. The Spaniel had stayed with him for weeks, digging holes around him to curl in, before finally giving up.

"The canines continue to blow me away," said Mike. "Each one teaches me a whole new set of things." He explained that Border Collies, like Journey, are not the preferred breed for search and rescue, but he and his wife are partial to the breed. "They're great once you get them dialed in, but training can be hard," he said. "They're really smart, but that can work against you. Journey would sometimes think, 'Oh, I can shortcut that.'" She was very toy-driven as a puppy which makes for a good search dog. As an enthusiastic puppy, she failed her first test when she alerted on a false hole, a hole that had not been spiked with human scent. That hasn't happened since. The handlers use training aids, such as items from a coroner's office, to reinforce the scent.

For the past two years, Mike and Journey have also been working with the Federal Emergency Management Agency, training on rubble, for example. She and Mike are part of the FEMA US&R Task Force #6. FEMA units are called out when large-scale events receive federal intervention. Although Journey used to wear a search dog vest, it's too dangerous for her to wear a collar or vest in disaster work because they might get hooked on something. Journey has never been injured in the field, but Mike can't say the same as he broke his ankle a few years back. From a liability and insurance standpoint, the Riverside County Sheriff's office has to approve all their missions. The OES will pay for lodging and fuel, but Mike ends up spending a lot of his own money for training, travel, and supplies.

Through March, they have been on a record 15 rescue missions so far this year. They are getting more exposure as a team and more callouts. Mike commented that too many people are spending time in the wilderness without proper preparation, such as telling someone where they are going, taking appropriate gear, and checking the weather. He said they've had to rescue people in Idyllwild who were out in 30-degree weather in shorts and T-shirts. "Also," he said, "if you get lost, just hunker down. We might be able to find you if you stop walking."

With the unsolved missing person cases, he said he tries to put them out of his mind. He said, "I'm a very busy person, and sometimes I spend too much time thinking. With Karlie, having a daughter myself, imagining not knowing where she is, it would be hard to live with that. Until you have some kind of proof, you can't rest."

Sugar

SUGAR works in Lisa's hair salon in Crowley Lake and at a construction workshop, greeting customers and raising people's spirits. The French Bulldog also serves as Lisa's constant companion, accompanying her to swim meets or to go shopping. Lisa recently drove to San Francisco, with Sugar riding shotgun the whole way.

At only one year old, she's extremely playful. She's crazy about balls and hustles a soccer ball around the backyard using her shoulder. She runs for any ball and can consistently bounce any-sized ball, from a little rubber ball to a gigantic exercise ball, off her nose. "If there's a misstep, it's because I threw it wrong," said Lisa.

This latter feat is remarkable because Sugar has only one eye. The breeder became aware that she was blind in one eye after the puppy's eyes opened at 10 days. Lisa had been waiting for a retired mommy bulldog, but she jumped at the chance to get Sugar. She explained that because Sugar never had the use of an eye, she easily compensates with her good eye. When she runs free, she just turns her head so the eye is in the middle of her sight. "She doesn't miss it," said Lisa.

That said, French Bulldogs are not known for their athleticism. They are descended from a sub-family of Mastiffs that was used for bull-baiting. When the sport was outlawed, English bulldogs became fashionable as companion dogs. They were cross bred with terriers to reduce their size and were exported to France where they were particularly popular with French lacemakers to keep their laps warm while they sewed. ". . . If you believe the folklore," said Lisa.

Frenchies are the sixth most popular dog breed in the US and are known for their playfulness and comical behavior. "She's definitely the house clown," said Lisa. "Plus she has no manners. She jumps on everybody and wants to sit in their lap." Because of Sugar's nature and her friendly face, Lisa says she has never met a child who was afraid of her. "Everyone wants to hold her like a stuffed animal. People miss her when she's not at work," she said. She also helps break the ice with people Lisa doesn't know. "She puts a smile on their faces," said Lisa. "If they're having a bad day, that fades away.

Although some French Bulldogs don't bark a lot, that is not how Sugar rolls. She's a big communicator, amusing people with her big deep bark and rumbles. She's also got some swagger, making her desires known, whether it's time to eat or time to play with a crunched-up water bottle that she carries proudly around the living room.

Sugar is well named because she is super friendly. She's very affectionate and will take any opportunity to lick and nuzzle. "She loves everybody, and everybody loves her," said Lisa. "We've never had a dog like her."

Jennie Roux

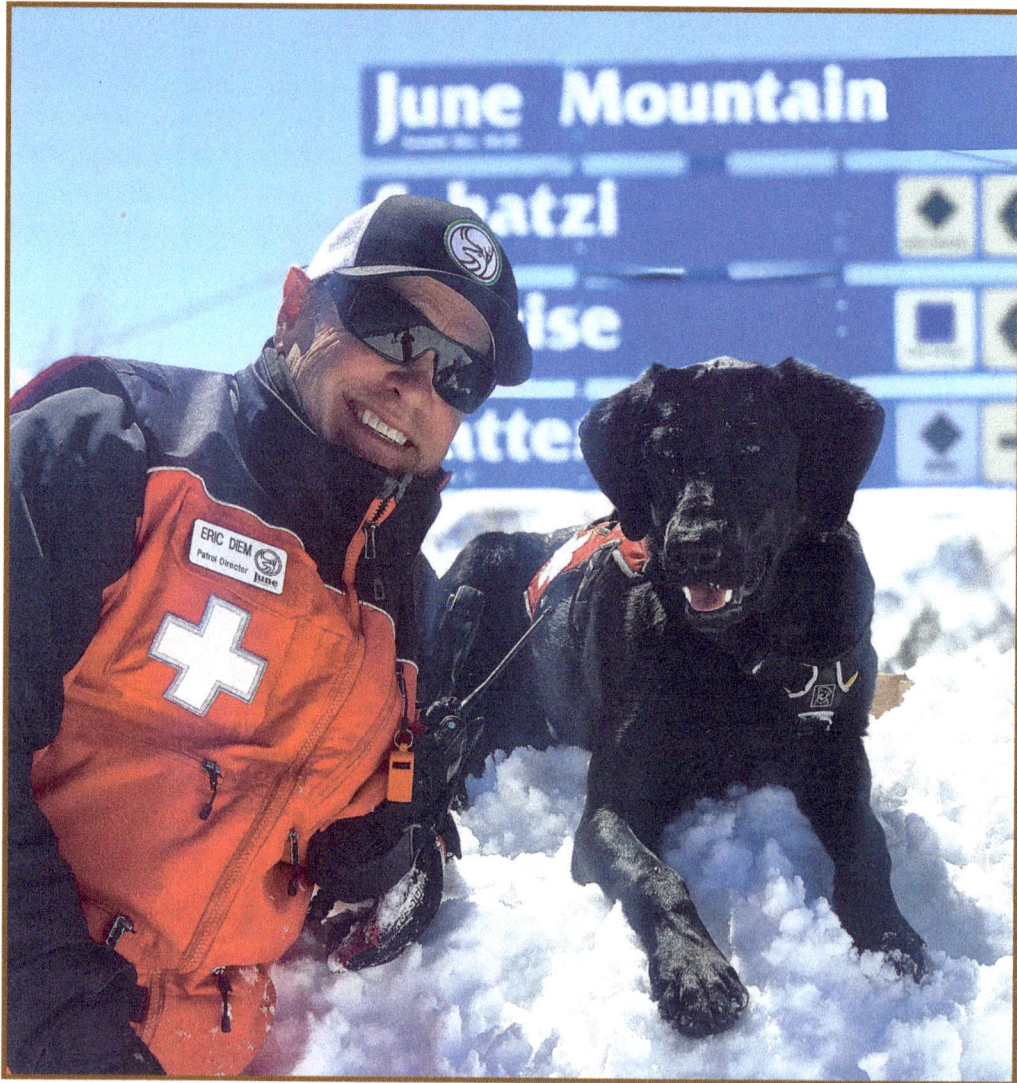

IT'S a beautiful bluebird day on June Mountain. Kids are everywhere, racing through the terrain park, skittering through the trees, and riding up the J1 lift to the lodge perched up high, overlooking the quaint town and two lovely lakes. But something is amiss. "Search, Jennie!" orders Eric, chief patroller. The Mountain's black Labrador avalanche dog goes to work. The children's voices fade as she concentrates. Guided by Eric's arm signals, she works a grid pattern, first across and then up and down. She focuses on terrain traps, such as tree wells, where a skier or snowboarder can get buried and suffocate within minutes. With her nose low to the snow, she works fast but is careful to thoroughly cover the area.

Then she finds it. Using her amazing ability to detect different odors, she picks up on a human smell coming from down in the snow. Her tail wagging furiously, she begins to dig with her big paws. The humans join in, and they dig carefully to avoid further injuring the body buried in the snow. Sure enough, they uncover a man lying still.

But then he moves! He pulls himself free of the snow. It's a patroller who volunteered to be buried so that Jennie could practice finding someone. "Thanks, Jennie," he says and pats her on the head. She is delighted to see her friend, and especially happy to see her flying squirrel toy which was buried with him. Eric throws the toy, and Jennie races after it, snow flying. Kids gather to hail the hero dog; they ruffle her fur, pull her ears, and breathe in her face. Jennie doesn't mind. The smile on her face seems to say, "The more love the better. Bring it on!"

Jennie Roux comes from Jenner's Run, a prestigious board and training facility in Colorado that sometimes has litters of Labrador Retriever puppies. It is owned and operated by Ann Wichmann, Colorado's first female park ranger. A search and rescue team member referred Eric to her and said she had the best Labs in the country. She is renowned for her expertise in training and certifying water, cadaver, and avalanche dogs, particularly for disaster work. She and her dogs have responded to multiple search emergencies, such as 9/11. Eric and his wife drove to Colorado to visit the operation and then had to spend the night so Ann could convince herself they were suitable. Having passed muster, they brought Jennie home, the only black Lab in the litter of six. She was eight weeks old. Now, nearly two, she has participated in over 30 training burials.

Back on the mountain, Eric is bundled up in multiple layers, coats, gators, helmet, and sunglasses to cope with the elements, but Jennie is at ease as she is. Her waterproof bi-layered coat keeps her warm and dry. The fur on her feet is short, so snow doesn't cling to them. At the end of the day, Jennie rides on the snowmobile, her tongue hanging out, sweeping the hill with Eric, to pick up any stragglers. As she surveys the kids and enjoys the ride, her expression says, "*This* is the best life for a dog!"

Dot, Great Pyrenees, and Many Border Collies

THE Echenique family takes the concept of working dogs to a whole new level. They have seven Great Pyrenees as guard dogs and about 12 Border Collies to herd sheep. "Yeah, we have a lot of dogs," Patti said. "We need dogs to manage the dogs," she joked. She has taken as many as 11 dogs at a time to get their shots at the local clinic. "I try to recruit friends," she said. It takes a lot of organization to keep that many dogs up to date, but it's required for the kennel permit and important because the Great Pyrenees sometimes roam.

Two males once disappeared and were discovered 12 miles away, guarding someone else's band. "Oh, they'll take care of anyone's sheep," said Patti. "They don't care." The big white dogs are not to be messed with. A mountain lion started coming around helping himself to a sheep out of the corral every day. The California Department of Fish and Wildlife tried to trap him with no luck. They installed a camera, but never saw a shadow of the big cat. They did capture lots of footage of the Great Pyrenees prowling around the sheep to protect them. Great Pyrenees are somewhat nocturnal and sleep all day before they go on duty at night. As flock guardians, they keep away coyotes, bears, and mountain lions. "They only bark for a reason. When you hear that big deep woof woof, you know something's out there," said Patti.

"The Pyrenees are less trainable than the Collies," she said. "They're more instinctual." The Pyrenees puppies are put in with the lambs so they learn to bond with them. The flock is really the Pyrenees' family. Because of their responsibilities, the Pyrenees are mostly kept away from people and are not treated as pets though Patti sneaks in a little socializing. "The puppies are so cute, sometimes you can't help yourself," she said. A very old breed, Great Pyrenees grow to weigh over 100 pounds and have an independent streak because they need to make decisions on their own.

One day, the sheep were bedded down for a siesta near Shady Rest Park. The shepherd and Joe, Patti's husband, were inside a nearby trailer, eating lunch. Suddenly, there was a big dustup, and the dogs were all barking. It turned out a jogger had run right through the middle of the sleeping sheep, startling a Great Pyrenees who reacted instinctively and bit him in the behind. The jogger was not pleased, and the police got involved, as well as animal control. The dog had to be quarantined for 10 days, but the authorities ultimately pointed out the dog was just doing its job, calling it a "justifiable bite." "It was kind of silly," Patti said. But she worries that the many cross country teams that train at Shady Rest don't know how to behave near sheep. "We should put up a sign that says 'Stay back' and 'Don't throw rocks,'" she said. "Those runners don't wear much protective gear."

The Echeniques run a large sheep operation that summers near Toms Place and Mammoth Lakes, and the flocks are often visible from US Highway 395 from June to November before the sheep are moved to Kern County for the winter. Joe's family has a long history in Mono and Kern counties and has been grazing sheep in Long Valley since the 1960s. They employ five to six shepherds who each handle a band of about 1,000 sheep aided by multiple Border Collies, all owned by the Echeniques. The shepherds are Peruvian and often give the dogs Spanish names and teach them to respond to Spanish commands. "Our dogs get to be bilingual," Patti said. "Of course, it's also a lot of whistles."

The shepherds come for three years on an agricultural visa and then have to return home for a period of time before they can come back. Because of changes with Homeland Security, it's gotten harder for the men to return to work. The Echeniques have been working with one Peruvian for more than 15 years and have employed his brother and cousins. Coming from the Andes Mountains, they like the Sierra, and shepherding allows them to send money home. Patti recounts the time she went to pick up a returning shepherd who was bringing his brother to the US for the first time. The first shepherd walked off the bus in jeans, plaid shirt, and boots. Then the little brother appeared in black slacks and loafers. "I immediately took him shopping," Patti said.

With regards to training the dogs, Patti said they don't do a lot. "I'll work them in the corrals and try to teach them manners, but mostly we put the younger dogs in with the older ones. That's how they learn." Sometimes it takes a dog a long time to mature. One dog didn't start watching sheep until he was three. Patti keeps some of the dogs with her in Nevada, and they get the winter off. "We have working dogs, and we have naughty dogs, which are mine," she chuckled.

Dot, one of the Border Collies, doesn't get off so easy. Dot belongs to Joe, "unless I'm around," Patti said, "then she ignores him." She described how, when she arrives after an absence, Dot will see her arrive from her kennel and practically bowl Joe over when he lets her out, so she can rush in the house to greet Patti. "She latches onto me and my dogs," Patti said.

The sheep are moved several times a year in trucks that are four-story sheep-mobiles. It's a big job to get the sheep into the corrals and up the loading chute. Similarly, when the sheep need tending, they have to be moved into holding corrals so they can get shots, treatments, or paint branded. Dot is indispensable in keeping the operations moving efficiently. "She's always watching," said Patti. "When I walk back to let more in, she knows what she's supposed to do." Dot will also round up any wandering sheep, which happens more in Mono County where the sheep roam free. In Kern County, the sheep are fenced, but they face another danger: trespassing dogs. "It's a bigger problem in Bakersfield," Patti said. "A pack of dogs will definitely kill sheep." The Great Pyrenees come to the rescue again. "A Pyrenees can take down a Rottweiler," Patti said.

With Collies in high demand for cattle and sheep herding in Mono County, puppies get traded around, and dogs are sometimes re-assigned. "We don't like the dogs to bite the sheep," Patti said. "It can cripple them." If they end up with a dog that bites, they'll try to find a cowboy to take it. "Cattle will put up more of a fight than sheep will," she said. "They need a more aggressive dog."

The Echeniques are of Basque heritage, and the Basques have a long tradition of sheepherding in the Eastern Sierra. There are fewer sheep now because of concerns that they carry diseases that endanger the native Sierra bighorn sheep, but if you do catch a glimpse of a flock, give a tip of the old *txapela* to the sheep, shepherds, and hard-working dogs.

Chief

AT 11, Chief is the veteran of the current avalanche rescue dogs on Mammoth Mountain, but Scott remembers well the circumstances of acquiring him. He said, "When we first started Eastside K-9, we didn't have much to go on other than puppies that came from a trusted line. Now we have aptitude tests for some inherent things, especially to distinguish between an alpha dog and a beta dog. We want a dog kind of in the middle, one with high drive but who will also get along with other dogs. These tests can help you start eliminating dogs left and right. You do not want an alpha, especially if it's your first dog, even for a pet."

Chief's mother was a therapy dog, and his dad was a hunting dog. "Right there, you've got some middle ground," said Scott. Because the black Lab was a big investment, Scott made several trips to visit the puppies. On his third trip, after a second puppy assessment, his decision was clear.

"The biggest thing is the prey/play test," he said. "We take the puppy out of his element, away from the litter, maybe on some nice grass, and pull out a brand new squeaky toy and start teasing him with it to see how he reacts. I thought all puppies would come over, but some are scared and run away. We want to see some confidence and inquisitiveness. Then we toss it a few feet away, remembering that they can't see very well at that age. Some will go get it and take it away, try to leave with it. Others will smell it and walk off. Ideally, they get it and bring it back to you. Those are the ones that want to interact with you."

They also test the puppies' reactions to loud noises, banging pots and pans behind them, to see if they run away or get aggressive. "You want them just to turn and look at you," Scott said. They also roll the puppy on its back and hold it down for a few moments. Beta dogs will just lie there; alpha dogs may start immediately struggling and biting. Middle dogs will have a reaction somewhere between the two.

Scott brought Chief home at 10 weeks and started training right away. "You start bonding with the dog, good eye contact, so they can read facial expressions. A stern look or happy look can go a long way," he said. "You don't have to raise a hand or yell. Just give them a mean look." Ideally, the puppy goes through basic obedience and potty training before the snow comes. "We need them well past all that when they show up for work," Scott said. "It's incredibly important to get exposed to different surfaces and machinery. We have quads, snowmobiles, metal grates, concrete, rocks, logs, helicopters, snow cats; it's a lot of stimulus for them."

The team starts by playing hide and seek in the woods. In the first phase, the searches are visual. The primary handler runs off with the puppy's reward toy and hides behind a tree while the secondary handler restrains the puppy who is watching everything. When the secondary handler yells "Search!" and releases the puppy, it goes tearing after the handler. Then there's a big party, loud praise, and the primary handler repeats the activated word, "Good search, Chief." Scott said, "You do that three times in a row, and you might do that every day for a week. They learn quicker when it's all high energy. We've never had a puppy not start off just blazing."

In the next phase of the game, the secondary handler tries to keep the puppy's eyes covered while the primary handler hides. "You set it up for success. Maybe it got a little glimpse. You do it on a day with a nice gentle breeze, and the person's scent will be easy for the dog to pick up from the direction of the release point. When the dog is released this time, it tears off but quickly realizes it doesn't know where to go. When it pauses, you see the nose go up, and it catches the scent and charges toward its new best friend. Sometimes it will sit there, with its head in the air, until it catches the scent. You do that three times with lots of energy. Then you keep elevating from there," Scott said.

Chief learned to use his nose really well. As a puppy, he would lead the rest of the litter to the food bin and open up the Rubbermaid container. He's also really good at getting out of his kennel. "We also give them the freedom to get their creative juices flowing. We encourage them to be inquisitive," Scott said. He described how Chief discovered a duffel bag in the ski patrol office, opened the zipper with his teeth, and shoved his nose inside to check it out.

Chief has been certified by the National Search Dog Alliance and passed the test of the prestigious Canadian Avalanche Rescue Dog Association. "We believe their standards are the highest in the world," said Scott. The dogs start with what Trico's handler, Steve, described as a Swiss-style of training, where live people are buried for the dogs to find. The dogs then advance to more of a Canadian challenge where scented articles are buried. Scott explained that Area Field search and rescue dogs find a scent and run back to their handler to alert. With avalanche work, time is crucial, and it would be a waste of time to re-find the scent, so avalanche dogs are trained to alert by staying by the site wagging their tail, barking, and digging. This is called "victim loyalty" in the avalanche industry. It's very hard to pull the dog away, and it will become aggressive if another dog tries to claim the hole. Multiple articles are buried, so there are enough for all the dogs. Outside of test situations, all the people Chief has found have been deceased. "It's not hero work," said Scott, "but it brings a conclusion to the family which is important."

Chief also mentors the new dogs. When the puppies see him playing "the game," they want to play too. "They're like a pack. They learn from each other," said Scott. "The whole patrol family, we're a pack too." Steve said, "That's one of the reasons we have the program we do, everyone brings a different perspective." Scott added, "We learn from each other. We watch and observe. Hopefully we learn all good habits."

Rusty

"I wasn't so sure of him at first. He didn't really show any interest in the cattle until he was about one," Leo said. "And then a light bulb came on. He barked a little at first too when he didn't have his confidence yet. He felt like he needed to make himself bigger. Now, he's really quiet. He just eyes them." He explained that barking can make the cows defensive and protective of their calves, and then they won't move, whereas a strong quiet presence keeps the herd calm. He said, "That keeps things from getting riled up. Sometimes the young ones go in there, kamikaze style, and you don't have control."

That can lead to someone getting hurt. He said Rusty's one-year-old daughter recently got kicked in the head by an irritated bull. "She went tearing in there to see what was going on, and the older dog forgot to tell her, 'Hey, I'm about to bite this bull, you better get out of the way.'" Something like that can ruin a young dog. Leo said, "They might still have that instinct, but they don't work like they're supposed to. They're like, 'We quit. This isn't as much fun as we thought.'"

Rusty is a three-year-old red Border Collie. "I wasn't a big fan til I got one. Now they're my favorite," Leo said. He was around Heelers as a kid, but they want to drive the cattle. "The dog's main deal is to bring them, just bunch them up, and let you drive," he said. Because the dogs are so fast, he said they can save a ton of horse and manpower. "Having a good dog is better than four guys," he said.

He turns the dogs by voice commands: "away" for right, "go by" or "by" for left. Leo said, "One guy I work with, he gets them mixed up, so he just yells 'right!' 'left!'" The dogs figure it out. Sometimes the dogs are too far away to hear him, so Leo also uses a dog whistle, one quick sharp toot for "stop and listen," two short for "left," and one long one for "right." And sometimes he forgets the whistle in the truck, so he just uses arm signals. "Usually, they know what we're doing anyway. They just watch me," he said.

Collies make good sheep and cattle dogs because they don't bark too much and are very smart, but that can work against them. Leo said, "The older dogs, after ten years, they know what you're going to do in a certain spot, but sometimes they try to outguess you. You have to say, 'That's not the plan today.'" Rusty is getting to where he can anticipate the next move. "Wherever I need him to be, he's just there," said Leo.

"It's amazing how fast they figure out when to be aggressive and not," he said. He had one dog though that was too tough. "He'd go in there at 100 miles per hour and just bite the cattle and hang on. We don't need that." It's hard to break a dog of that. He sent him to a buddy who uses dogs to hunt wild cattle. "That dog needed a different job," he said.

"Our cows are dog-broke," he explained. Cows that haven't been around dogs all their lives are likely to see dogs as attackers, like coyotes. They might charge a dog from 100 yards away and can stomp it or hem it against a bush. Like experienced cattlemen, dogs learn to anticipate when they work with cows like that. "They learn to read cattle," said Leo. "They can see her looking and tell she's gonna make that move." Good dogs that is. Leo is moving cattle this week, bringing in the calves to get vaccinated and branded. That work requires a lot more guys on horseback. "Everyone has a dog," said Leo. "Some of them, you wish they'd been left at home."

He tries to evaluate a puppy's potential by seeing how it plays with a flag tied to a whip, if it ignores it or tries to tear it to shreds. "It's hard to tell," he said. He had a couple puppies that never showed an interest in herding. "There'd be cattle around. They didn't even care," he said. Some people start their puppies herding ducks or goats in a pen. "The key is to get them in position and then stop them," Leo said. He learns from other trainers and incorporates new things in his own puppy training. "It's pretty interesting," he said.

Being a cattle dog is dusty, thirsty, dangerous work. "It's a problem. By the time they get really good, they get hurt or killed. You're constantly having to start over," said Leo. He rotates four dogs to rest them and reduce their risk of being run over, rolled, or kicked. On the other hand, as part of the Lacey Livestock operation, they work all up and down beautiful Owens Valley from Olancha to Bridgeport, from high desert to meadow country. "It's a great life," said Leo.

Tara

SOMETHING didn't add up. The California Highway Patrol Officer had stopped the guy on US Highway 395 for speeding, but he was acting strangely. He first said he was going to stay a few days with family in Reno, but he didn't have any luggage. Then his story shifted, and shifted again.

Puzzled and suspicious, the CHP officer stepped away and called Mammoth Lakes Police Officer Hansen and his narcotics dog, Tara. They arrived with Tara riding in the back of Officer Hansen's police car on a platform he had built for her. Tara was delighted to have a chance to work and circled the speeder's car excitedly. Then she caught a big whiff of something she had been trained to detect. She jumped up and began scratching enthusiastically at the trunk. Inside was a tire changing kit, smeared with axle grease. And inside that was a kilo of heroin.

Officer Hansen had always had a goal to be a K-9 handler. He was highly motivated to get drugs off the street, and an alert dog seemed like a good tool to achieve that. He also thought it would be fun to work with a dog. Tara, a Belgian Malinois, was an experienced narcotics dog when she arrived in Mammoth. She had been working with the Mono County Sheriff's Department for three years after starting her career in New Mexico. Several trainers observed that she was one of the best alert dogs they had ever worked with.

"Finding drugs was really her thing," said Officer Hansen. "She would come out of the car going 100 miles per hour." With traffic stops, if he didn't take her out of the car right away, she would start barking because she wanted to get to work, or, in her mind, come play the game. He wasn't surprised when she found several trash bags full of marijuana in one car, but he was impressed when she found a tiny meth pipe in a sealed plastic bag in a glove box.

Tara was trained to detect marijuana, methamphetamine, cocaine, heroin, and "ecstasy." She worked with Officer Hansen for a year and a half before the laws regarding marijuana changed, abruptly ending her career. "You can't retrain a dog to forget the smell of marijuana. Once imprinted, they will always remember," Officer Hansen explained. Having a dog potentially alert on a legalized substance takes away the justification for a search and presents a liability in court. Tara was retired early, and Officer Hansen purchased her so she could live out her days comfortably. Sadly, as often happens with working dogs when they retire, Tara began to go downhill, and soon she was gone.

Officer Hansen has many fine memories of her, not only of her work ethic, but also of her sense of humor. In the police station, she would pretend to favor his boss, sneaking over to sleep by his chair or strolling to the sergeant's car when they got called out. "It was a running joke between us," said Officer Hansen.

Although Tara had been trained as a patrol dog, to potentially move into action if the officer were threatened, she was good around people, enjoying their foot patrols around the Village mall, greeting adults and kids. "Everyone wanted to meet the dog," said Officer Hansen. "She was a good ambassador for the department." He added, "Plus I just loved her."

Smalls the Singer

WHEN Devin's Chihuahua passed away suddenly from a heart attack, she was heartbroken. She stopped by the Whitmore Shelter to see if she could maybe walk a dog and feel better. A new dog had arrived, a transfer who was suffering from depression. He didn't want to be touched and was especially leery of men, but he came to Devin and sat on her lap.

He was tiny, about seven pounds, and only a year old. The shelter staff thought he was a Chihuahua mix. When Devin brought him home, her mother looked him over and said, "It looks like they took all the extra parts from other dogs and put them together." They called him Leftover for a while before settling on Smalls.

Then Devin discovered he had a hidden talent. She was talking to him one day in a sing-song voice, and he started crooning back at her. It turns out Smalls can sing, and not just briefly. He can vocalize for over half a minute, in a variety of howls, barks, chirps, growls, and warbles. It's a riot and can make anyone laugh.

Smalls suffers from stage fright however and doesn't like to go out in public, so he prefers to display his talent in the privacy of his home. But he sings every day to keep his vocal chords in shape. Videos of his performances are popular on the internet, and he has many fans.

True to his diva persona, he is a very fussy eater and is selective about the company he keeps. He favors new toys to old, but his bed is his favorite place to burrow and hide. He enjoys walks but doesn't like snow. He thinks it's nasty and cold, and he prefers to vacation in Arizona.

Devin discovered that he also has some serious athletic agility which makes him almost cat-like. He can spring three feet in the air and land on a bar stool. When given a treat, he'll execute a series of twirls and spins in delight. He perches on her shoulder like a parrot and stares into the computer screen while she's working.

His goofy charm has made him a Crowley favorite. He is protective of his home and leaps onto a windowsill to peer out at anyone who rings the doorbell. And, of course, barks.

Willow

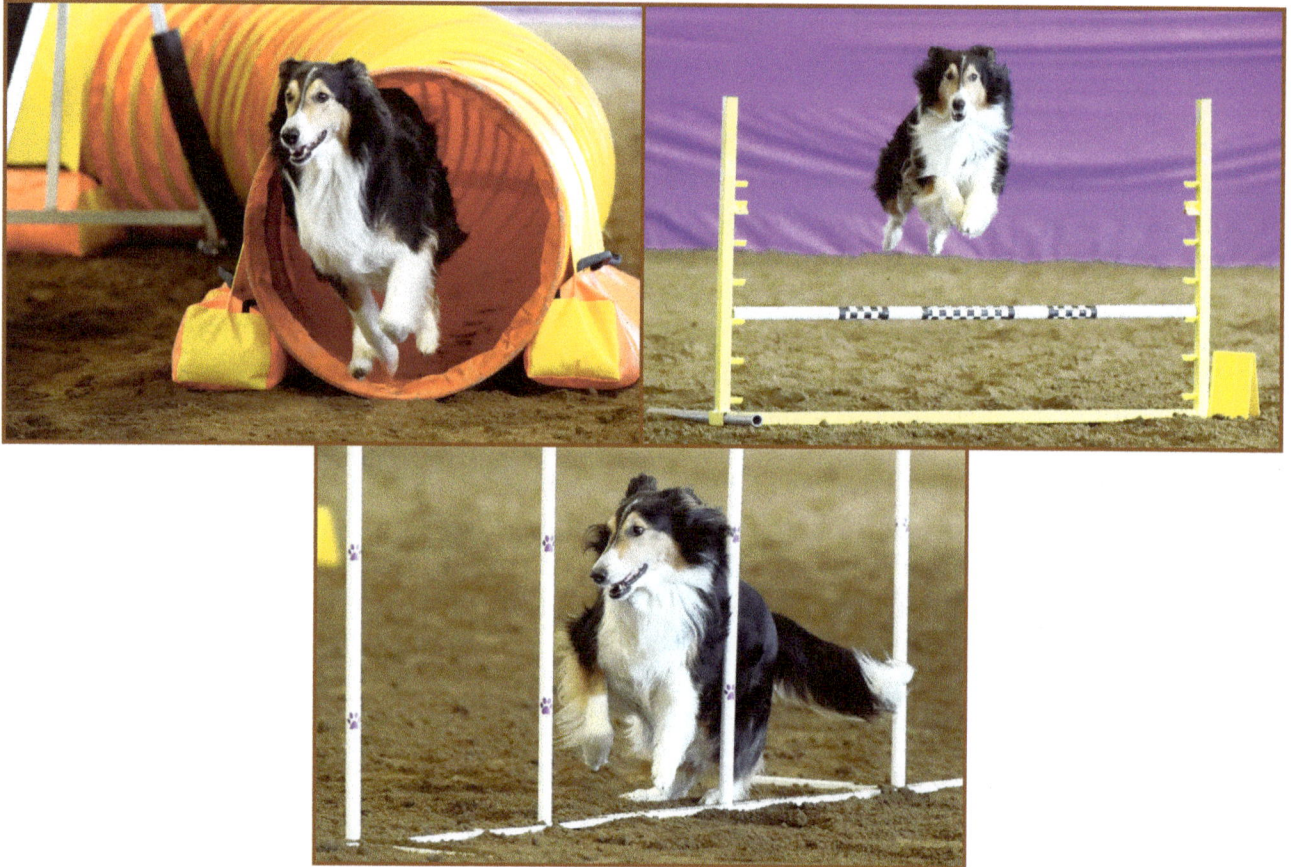

THIS is Willow, jumping, running, and dashing through the weave poles so fast she's a blur to the naked eye. She has placed second, third, or fourth in the nation in the Collie category in each of the last five years. "At almost 12 years old, she's still out there killing it," said her trainer Lynne.

The kind of agility practiced in Bishop and Mammoth is one designed for trainers of a wide range of ages and physical abilities. "We have older people in our group, even a stroke survivor," said Lynne. Some handlers choose to run with their dogs on a course, like the sprinting trainers in running shoes sometimes seen on television. Others are able to stand in a 10-by-10-foot area guiding their dogs around a course of up to 30 obstacles in a 100-by-100-foot ring, using verbal and physical cues. It can look like magic to a bystander as the dog seems to read the mind of its trainer and races through, over, and under an array of jumps, dog walks, weave poles, hoops and tunnels. The obstacles require athleticism on the part of the dog, but most of the challenge lies in the ability of the trainer and dog to work as a team.

As a nascent agility trainer, Lynne started looking for a herding dog and found one at a shelter in Colorado. She made the long drive, "because we're crazy," she said, and returned home with Sage. Not six months later, she received a call from a dog foster parent who excitedly told her, "I think I found Sage's sister! She's a dead ringer for her." Another long drive and a DNA test later, it was confirmed: Lynne now had two siblings, Sage and Willow.

But psychologically, Willow was damaged. It's hard to know what had happened to her, but she was terrified of everyday things, like a hose hanging on a neighbor's house. "She would just start screaming," said Lynne. She began reading about dogs' brains and how to build confidence in a dog. Agility was a big part of Willow's recovery. Now, as she flies around the trial course like the champion she is, you'd never know that she suffered from anxiety. "Sometimes I can tell she's feeling a little nervous before an event," said Lynne. "But no one else would notice."

When Lynne moved to the Eastern Sierra, twenty-plus years ago, she looked around for some agility classes to participate in with her dog at that time, but no one knew more than she did. She picked up a few pieces of equipment and put what she had learned from her limited experience to work. Now, she and another local trainer offer beginning classes in agility. "People sometimes think their dog would be good at agility because it can jump, but the teamwork with the trainer is more important," she said. They use a form of training called "shaping," which relies on reinforcement of desired behavior, explained by the adage "Never wrong, sometimes more right." Lynne said, "Occasionally, a dog seems to think, 'This is stupid; I don't see the point,' but most dogs enjoy a mental challenge. If we assume that all they think about is dinner, we're underutilizing our dogs. It's amazing to see the bond that can develop if it's fostered a bit. To go out on a course and showcase everything you've worked out together can really be something."

The trainers learn as much as the dogs. "Seeing the lightbulb go off when they've figured something out is rewarding," Lynne said. She's also amused when she sees agility training carry over into someone's everyday life. She said, "It's about learning to be patient and creative, looking at a problem from a different perspective. Sometimes you see the positive in an outcome even if it wasn't your goal."

Johnny and Oso

THE pack races through the trees, feet pounding and tongues lolling out of their mouths. They are on a remote trail on US Forest Service land, far from any roads or people or other dogs. Off leash, they are free to run, socialize, explore, and check out the amazing landscape. They leave the trees and gather on a high granite ledge with views of the Sierra crest and lakes below. This isn't your ordinary dog walking service.

Sierra Dog Ventures launched two years ago when owners Christi and Duncan moved to Mammoth Lakes and began experimenting with off-leash dog adventures. "This town is so incredible," she said. "People and dogs were willing to give it a try." Controlling a pack of up to 17 dogs in the wilderness is no walk in the park. Fortunately Christi and Duncan can lean on their two dogs, Johnny and Oso.

"They're good mediators," said Christi. "Oso is really tuned into the other dogs." The three-year-old Rottweiler German Shepherd mix will notice if one dog is being picked on and will push the bully dog away. He also has several girlfriends in the pack whom he entertains with kisses and flirtations along the trail. "Oso is all love all the time," she said.

She calls Johnny her "tiger dingo," due to his Shetland Sheep Dog breeding and stripes on his face. He's more reserved, but his herding instincts are evident in his ability to keep the pack together and nip at the heels of the laggards.

Christi explained that, as pack leaders, her dogs help the other dogs feel more secure. "Dogs are always ready for another dog to show them the way if they're unsure," she said. "Our dogs listen to us and respect us, and that makes the other dogs feel more confident."

She also noticed how off-leash freedom affects the dogs' confidence. She said some dogs show a lot of aggression when they are leashed that disappears when they are running free. "Freedom really does something to a dog's psyche," she said. Johnny used to exhibit considerable anxiety when they lived in Southern California, and that has decreased a lot. "Of course, the exercise helps," she said. The humans cover eight miles a day, and the dogs turn that into 10 to 15.

Christi said she learns more about dog behavior every day. The remarkable thing for her was to watch how dogs quickly integrate into the pack. "It's so profound to me how they just immediately accept each other as friends, regardless of breed," she said. "Even when one dog has kind of a funky energy, and I see the others don't really like him that much, they're still like, 'We're all in this together. Let's just go have fun.'"

Oso is the same sweet dog he was down south, but now when Christi asks him if he's ready to go to work, he howls with happiness. She said that the dogs' excitement when they pile out of the truck to start their adventure is contagious. "Whatever is going on in your head, it's impossible to be in a bad mood," she said. "That's the thing I love the most—their joy."

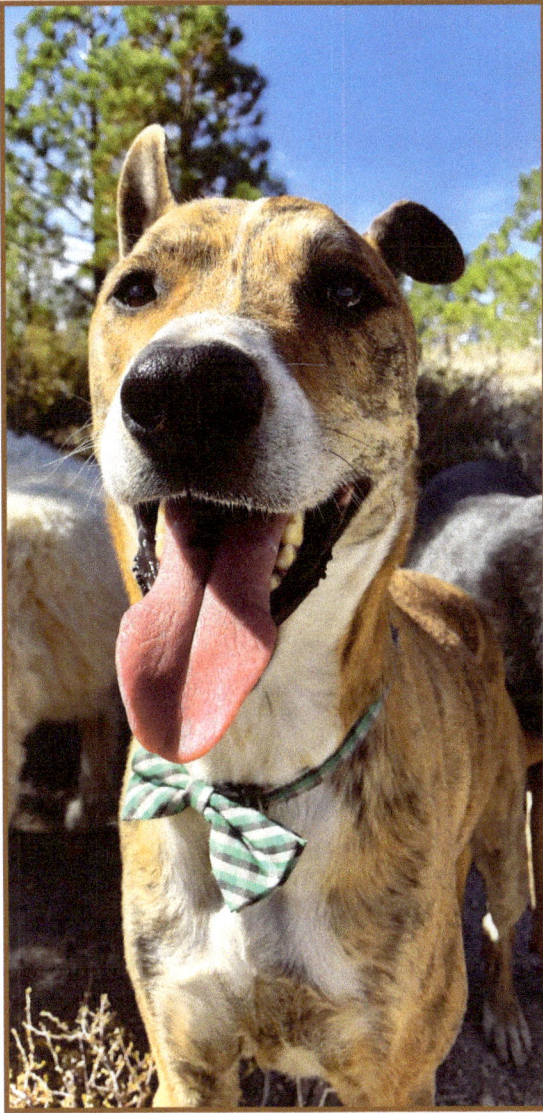

Bella

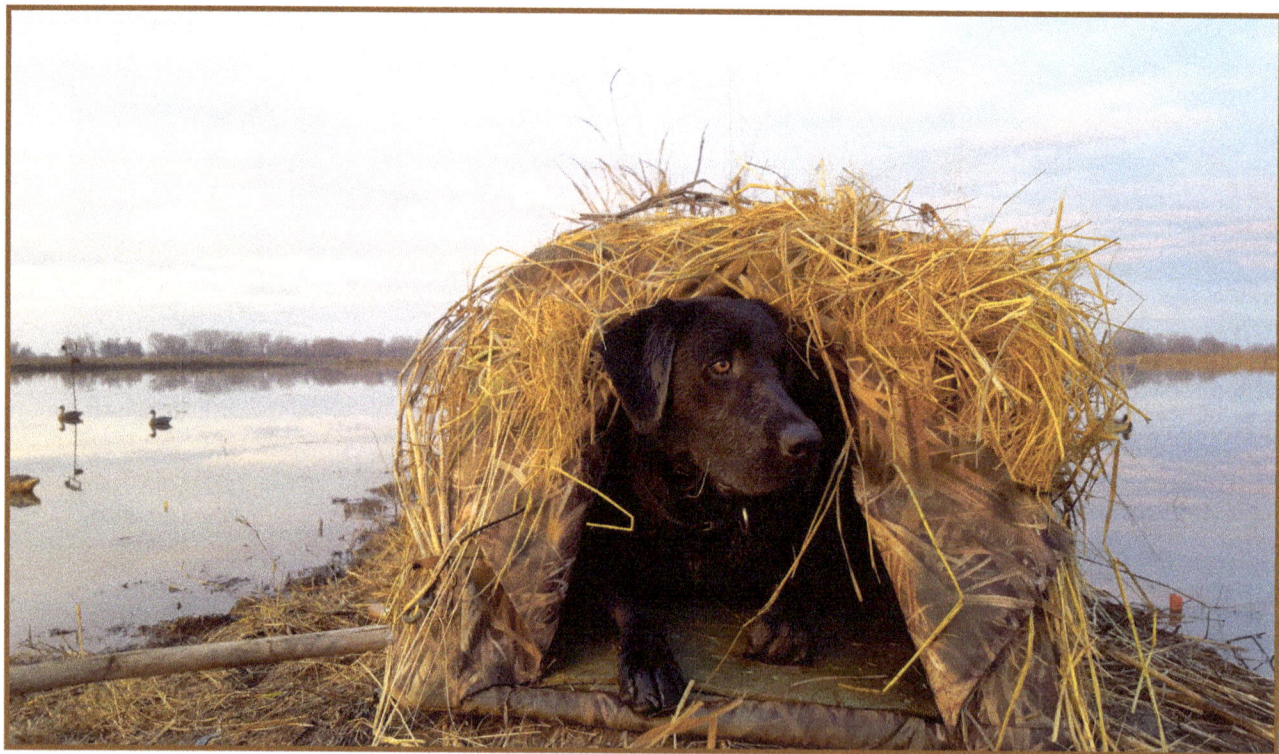

WHEN Eric put a deposit down for a new black Lab puppy, he didn't realize he would be getting the pick of *two* litters, a total of 16 puppies. "I spent a whole lot of time over there whittling it down from 16 to 14, 12, 8, 4, 2 and finally one," he said. The one was Bella who is now five years old. "I couldn't be happier with her," he said.

He explained that the Bishop breeder had done a really good job, using dams and sires from out of town and then doing all the modern tests: DNA to check for mutant genes, X-rays on elbows and hips for dysplasia, and checking their eyes for degenerative conditions. "Mutant gene issues are showing up more frequently in Labs due to poor breeding practices. EIC, Exercise-Induced Collapse, is one that affects Labs. A young Lab may not display symptoms initially, and you could be out working them one day, and, boom, they just fall over. They'll probably live, but you can't work them anymore," Eric said. "The science is at that level now. People who don't take advantage of these tests are doing a disservice to the dogs and the breed."

In search of a puppy he could train to be a bird dog, he picked Bella because of her drive. "I was looking for that alertness, that desire to chase a wing or ball thrown across the yard, that competitive drive to chase and grab ahead of her litter mates," he said. At seven weeks, Bella began kindergarten, with basic obedience. Eric began training her with puppy-oriented bird decoys. Once she retrieved the decoy, he would call her and gently coax her back to him on her check cord (a long leash). She didn't know to let go of the decoy, so he would put a little pressure on her gum and teeth to get her to drop it in his hand. "She had to learn that it's my bird, not hers," he explained.

Bird hunters guide their dogs with a combination of voice commands, hand signals, and whistles. One whistle means "sit and look for further instruction." Two whistles mean "go the direction I'm pointing," and a trill means "come back." Eric explained you start the training by having the dog sit and then blow the whistle. After enough iterations, when you blow the whistle, the dog will sit down. It's very important that the dog knows to sit and stay still. "Especially if you're in the blind, birds are landing, guns and people everywhere, you don't want her walking out in front of you," he said.

Whistles work better than voice commands because they carry farther. Bella has to know to look back after the first whistle to get the hand signal, either left or right or straight back before she gets the "go" signal. "You have to keep the wind in mind, to use that nose for finding the game," Eric said. "People ask me if I give her a treat when she gets it. Nah, her reward is the retrieve. She just wants to get the bird or dummy. She lives for that," he said.

Bella is competitive. "She'll go as hard as she can. She definitely doesn't want to be second to the bird, but she will always honor another dog's retrieve," Eric said. He said one of the reasons he hunts is to watch the dogs work. He and a friend took Bella and Avery, another black Lab, up to Canada to hunt with some friends from Idaho. Eric tells the story: "We dropped a couple geese, one at 70 yards, one at 90 yards. The dogs brought back the one at 70, and my buddy starts to walk out there to get the other one. I said, 'Hey, I didn't haul my dog all the way from California so you could walk out there and get that bird.' I sent Bella out. I knew she was going to go to the first spot. When she got there, I blew the whistle, and she sat down. I gave her the hand signal and whistle to

go further out. She went right to that far bird, picked it up, and brought it back to me. The guy goes, 'We got a well-trained dog here!'" Eric added, "But don't ever try to show off with them though. Then they won't do a thing right."

The dogs also have to get used to the guns. "You start off by shooting a little cap gun while they're eating. They'll be like, 'Whatever, don't bug me, I'm eating.' Then, you shoot the gun when they're pretty far away so they don't get scared, then you move them closer and closer, until you're shooting it off right next to them," he said. Bella now gets excited when Eric brings out the gun or training dummies. "She'll be lying around the house, thinking, 'Man, I never get to do anything.' Then you bring the gun out, and she gets fired up. When you're hunting, she's on it, really enjoyable to watch."

In the field, Bella works Upland game birds, ground birds like quail, chukar, pheasants, and Hungarian partridges, as well as water fowl. With the Upland birds, she works out in front of the hunter to find and flush the birds. She also watches where the birds fall, assuming Eric doesn't miss. "Oh, she'll give you a dirty look if you miss," he said. "Like, 'Here I am doing all this work, and you mess up.'" With waterfowl, Eric sets up in his blind with Bella in her blind facing him. "She's good with her eyes," he said. "If something is flying behind me, she'll be tracking it with her eyes, and I'll look back and, sure enough, there'll be birds flying there." Bird dogs are also important in retrieving downed and crippled birds. Eric said, "If you cripple a bird, and it lands in a tule patch in the water or it runs off in the bushes, Bella can get downwind and find it."

Eric says he'll always have a black Lab. "They are such good companions, great family dogs, and, like most dogs, everything is unconditional with them. They're like, 'Whatever you need, Dad.'" He bred Bella a couple of years ago with the #4 national field trials dog, and a few of her children are still around town. "I get to babysit them sometimes and keep an eye on them. They have the same drive and energy that their mother has. I'm definitely going to get one of her grandchildren someday," he said. He's wise to plan ahead. "Dogs just don't live long enough. It's a terrible thing God did, to make our dogs' lives so much shorter than ours," he said. For now though, he's pretty thrilled with Bella. "Bella goes almost everywhere with me. I know that there are better bird dogs out there than her," he said, "but she's pretty special to me."

King

KING and Sean are known as the godfathers of the avalanche dog program at Mammoth Mountain, "It all started with them" is a common refrain. It actually started with Stanley, Sean's Border Collie. "That dog was crazy smart," said Sean. "I swear, if he'd had a thumb, I could have taught him to drive my truck." Stanley was born in the sage brush when his sheepherding mother and the sheep were on the move. Sean didn't do much formal training except teach Stanley to be his right-hand man, but the dog's instincts and wits impressed him.

Sean had been on Mammoth Mountain ski patrol for several years before he began thinking about starting an avalanche dog program. "Other ski areas already had dogs," he said, "and we had as much if not more avalanche danger." He started reading and talking to folks in the Tahoe area, and people were game to share their knowledge and provide support. "They were completely open. Their attitude was 'We're all doing the same thing, trying to help people, keep them from getting into situations that could be prevented.' They were a really big asset to the program, rather than me just trying to figure it out. We're pretty removed in Mammoth. My thinking was 'Who's going to keep us in check, make sure we're up on our standards?'" said Sean.

An advisor mentioned a litter of Golden Retrievers, sired by a Tahoe avalanche dog. "Goldens were high on my list," said Sean. "They have a good prey drive, and I thought people might like to see more of a teddy bear-looking dog for the first time on the mountain versus a German Shepherd or Malamute that might scare people." He drove up to check out the litter. He said, "We didn't have those little games, those trials, that we have now. I had a little bit of experience because years prior I'd worked with a police detective who had gotten his canine avalanche certified. I wasn't completely blind but pretty darn close to it." It didn't matter. A puppy followed him up the stairs and across the deck while he introduced himself to the owners. "They say, 'You don't pick your dog, your dog picks you.' That was true," he said. "I never questioned if I got the right dog."

Sean wrote a proposal for Mammoth Mountain to bring in an avalanche dog program. The Mountain was open to it. "It didn't take long before everything proved itself," said Sean. "King got certified, and we were working well as a team." Sean was motivated to provide a resource on the mountain but also to people who ski out of bounds. "We have quite a community who go off-piste. The dogs could help us if they get in trouble out there," he said. He also saw it as an opportunity for a ski patroller to advance in their career. "You can get stuck in a rut. The dog program adds a twist," he said.

The dogs are owned by their individual handlers who, as ski patrollers, are on the clock while they work with the dogs. "Some ski areas do own the dog, and, yes, it's a risk that you put all this effort in and people will just leave and take their dog with them. But we think that bond is important, and we're really careful to look for handlers who can make a long commitment. It's not for somebody who just wants to look cool with a dog on the mountain." said Sean. He said the handler also has to think about what the dog is exposed to. "You can't take them and do everyday things, like rock climbing or swimming in the river. Your bond is at such a high level, but you still have to look at them as a tool to save people's lives. They're working dogs. You can't expose them to something that could be career-ending. That dog needs to go in tomorrow at 100 percent," he said.

Establishing Eastside K-9, the nonprofit that supports the dogs, was an afterthought but turned out to be very important. "I knew that we were creating a really valuable asset in the dog, and I needed to have funds to outfit him, pay for his medical care, and insure him. I wanted a safety net for other handlers to not be financially exposed because of their dogs," said Sean. "They need to know that if something medically should be done for the dog, we'll take care of it, to avoid any resentment toward the program and to protect the dog." The nonprofit is funded by donations and, 15 years later, is going strong, with four dogs now in the program. The dogs are also supported by the Mountain and sponsorships, proudly sporting little badges on their vests.

Sean spent a lot of time thinking about what could go wrong and how to prepare the dog for it. He said, "King was always willing to do crazy stuff, hanging out of the gondola or being lowered from a chair lift. There was a lot of trust." Sometimes King's enthusiasm would catch Sean by surprise. "One day, he loaded onto Chair 11 ahead of me. I turned around, and he had already hopped on and taken off. We rode up to the top, me on the chair behind him, and at the top he jumped down when I called, 'Off,' and waited for me. He was highly trained at that point, but we hadn't done that before," Sean said.

Some training offered a chance to educate the public on the slopes. "Sometimes, I'd have to tell people 'We're working right now.' They can come by the patrol room later, to pet the dogs and take photos," he said. "I wanted people to look at the dogs the same way they look at ski patrol, as someone they can go to for help, as a trained resource. The thing is, the dogs put so much dedication into their work. I wanted them to be respected for that." Because the dogs get so much attention, it can be a distraction for the handler. "You get a lot of exposure, getting to be a rock star for the day. It puts you in the limelight. The key is to stay focused and remember you still have a job to do," he said.

He explained that distractions during training exercises are a good thing because it teaches the handler and dog how to stay on task. He said, "When you're on scene, the handler is multi-tasking. It's a lot of pressure. You need to delegate, you're searching with your transceiver, you're looking for hazards, watching out for a secondary avalanche, people coming in and contaminating the area. You have to be thinking about the wind and how you're working your dog. It's a lot to think about to manage the scene and can be a little overwhelming. That's why you train, so it doesn't become such a stressful situation."

He also said the training exercises can be a fabulous recruiting tool, for handlers and for puppies. "We let the pups watch when a senior dog goes into a training scenario. It's easy to sell it to a new pup. They want to play too," he said. "Potential handlers get interested too. It gets them excited about that part of the program." Overall he said the program is progressing well, with dogs and handlers rotating in as others leave. "People dig it," he said. "I've been really happy with it. It's worked out."

Gigi

GIGI is watching. Her eyes roam the skies, looking for ravens and hawks. She stares down the long driveway to see if strangers are approaching. She keeps an eye out for the pair of coyotes who have been hanging around. If she sees them, she uses her special coyote bark. She climbs up on a pile of snow to see even farther. She gazes over at her fellow canines and humans. It's her job to keep her herd safe.

Gigi is an Old-Time Scotch Collie, a Scotland breed imported to the US in large numbers in the 1880s to work on farms. Known for their intelligence and dependability, Collies grew in popularity in the twentieth century. The American Kennel Club eventually dropped the "Scotch" and adopted the terms "Rough" and "Smooth" to differentiate show dogs from the working, or Scotch, Collies. Scotch Collies are now somewhat rare though an organized effort is underway to bring back the breed.

She was born in Oregon. Her kaleidoscope coat is tri blue merle, a coloring shared by one other puppy in the litter of eleven. Crowley Lake resident Pam heard of the litter of Scotch puppies while she was traveling in France and selected the name Gigi because in French it means "trustworthy girl from the farm." Back in the US, Pam drove three days to pick up the pup. Now nine months old, Gigi weighs 43 pounds and is likely fully grown.

Unlike hunting dogs who are comfortable ranging far from their owners, herding dogs are sometimes called "velcro" dogs because they have an innate desire to stick close. Nevertheless, when Pam started training Gigi to hike off leash in the open public lands around Crowley, she was surprised Gigi had almost immediate recall, the ability of a dog to return to its owner when called even when exciting distractions like rabbits, birds, or other dogs are present. Now, Gigi can instantly pivot from chasing a bird at a dead run to circle back to Pam. Hiking companion dogs also must be friendly to other people and dogs. Dogs that don't get along can be a real problem off leash. Gigi is not shy, but she has an easy personality.

"She's a real thinker," said Pam. "She assesses things before she reacts." Gigi has started to train in agility, and Pam plans to pursue herding and possibly some scent work. Gigi has already learned a lot about agility by watching some trials on television. "It was hilarious. She just watched and watched," said Pam. Gigi enjoys watching TV from the family rocker recliner where she can study what's happening on the big screen. "You can definitely see the wheels turning," Pam said. Another day, coming back to the yard after a trip to the kitchen, she was amused to find Gigi sitting up in her Adirondack chair like a person.

Pam explained that the dogs need an outlet for their herding instincts. Besides livestock herding, another possibility is Treiball, a game where dogs compete to herd large inflatable balls into a net. That may be in Gigi's future, but for now, she's waiting for the snow to melt while she watches over her "flock."

Bell

THINGS didn't start well with Bell. She was already a year old when Edo got her, and when she arrived at the ranch, she took off after a coyote and started a fight. But Edo had learned that dogs that start off as goofballs can turn into great dogs. Two years later, after a huge investment of time and attention, she is turning into an effective cattle dog.

Edo starts his dogs on goats where he can teach the commands in a confined space, even beginning puppies as young as two to three months old. The goats are smaller than cows and less likely to injure a puppy. They're also calmer and won't panic and hurt themselves if the dog is too aggressive. And they're cheaper than cows if one does get hurt in a training session. "You can teach a dog a lot in a month. You want to stimulate it but also control it," he said. "You don't want the dog to get overexcited and just start chasing them around like cats."

He keeps his puppies either in a kennel or on a leash. "Everyone has different methods, but I keep mine constantly supervised. A puppy that gets out will find cows and start working them. It learns that it doesn't need you, and then it won't listen to you." he said. "Everything starts from very small things that are hard to observe, but you have to be mindful of. Then you build from that. You have to constantly watch your dog and always be aware of where it is, especially when it is young and eager. If you don't pay attention, it will get bad habits."

The dog has to learn to control the cattle. Edo said, "If a cow wants to go somewhere and you don't want that, the dog has to be able to stop it, but the cow is bigger and stronger. The dog has to be able to intimidate the cattle and hold the space. You have to use the right method or the cattle will win. If I see it's not working, I'll go help my dog. I want it to know we're a team." On the other hand, the dog can't scare the herd. "You can't put in a strong dog who is going to bite the cows. We like our cows; we want the dogs to be nice, not just kick them around. The cows must respect the dog, but not be afraid. If they get scared, they'll bunch up and face the dog, especially if there are calves. Then the dog can't move them. You also don't want to scare them into running. It's a fine balance."

Because the cattle are genetically bred and meticulously cared for to produce high quality beef, they are very valuable, and moving them is a serious endeavor. "It's not like in the movies, where—ycchaw!—they just take off," said Edo. "Now the market is really competitive, so what we do is very scientific and precise. We do a lot of planning to make sure that the move is do-able, that there is water, that the cows can handle it."

Similarly, he takes good care of his cattle dogs, keeping them hydrated and well fed. He has to watch for fatigue. "Bell is a trooper, but when she gets tired, she'll start doing things I don't want,

like trying to work where you're working because it's easier," he said. Border Collies have such a high drive for work, that they can injure themselves by overworking or overheating.

Bell is showing some natural ability in crowd control. "She knows when to lie down," Edo said. "Some dogs don't want to stop because they aren't confident that they can get the cows moving again." He has learned to be patient when it comes to dog training. He said, "I think she's going to get better. She's a lot of help, and I appreciate her for what she does."

Buster

"BLAME my wife," said Paul. "She's the one who wanted a Lab. I wanted a Heeler." As a young man, he was impressed with a Heeler owned by a co-worker, a guy from Louisiana. They worked on a dairy farm and would have to round up the cows. "There was all this liquid manure. It was disgusting work. My buddy goes, 'Hey, Blue, go get the cows,' and that little guy goes out there and gets all the cows, even the ones that were trying to hide. I thought that was pretty cool," said Paul.

Friends of his wife told her that she should insist on getting a Lab. "They told her, 'You work hard. You should get what you want,'" Paul said. "I said, 'That's true. Okay, let's go get a Lab.'" They went to a barn where a litter of Labs had been born in the hay. Buster was the last one left. "He was a little bit shy," said Paul. "He was an unwanted dog." Buster is now legendary in the Eastern Sierra because of his human decomposition detection abilities. Paul said, "Someone said there will never be another dog like him. That's true."

As a Mammoth Lakes police detective, Paul had been on the site of an avalanche on Mammoth Mountain and had been amazed at the speed and efficiency of the avalanche dogs. He observed, "A dog can search that area in minutes while it would take a really long time to do it with a probe line." He decided to train Buster as an avalanche dog at the same time Sean was working with King. For some reason the two dogs didn't get along, but their owners did. During Buster's first test, when the dogs were given 30 minutes to find two buried victims somewhere on one acre, Buster found them in about six minutes. Paul knew he had a special dog.

Buster proved to be an excellent avalanche dog. Fully trained, he shows his stuff in a YouTube video, when, in blizzard conditions, from 100 feet away, it takes him two minutes to locate a reporter who had been buried under four feet of snow. Then Paul started thinking about dead people. He began to train Buster to alert for the scent of chemicals released by human decomposition that can be detected decades, maybe hundreds, and some say, thousands of years after a burial, even deep underground or through concrete. "Finding fresh human remains is like kindergarten," Paul said. "Grave work? That's like grad school."

Paul's inspiration was Barker Ranch, home of the Manson Family near Death Valley at the time of their arrest for a spate of murders in 1969, including Sharon Tate's. Many clues, including testimonials and mysterious missing person cases, pointed toward the likelihood of bodies buried at the ranch. In all, Buster and Paul made over 20 trips to the site, with Buster alerting to human remains in multiple areas. They teamed up with two forensic anthropologists from Oak Ridge National Laboratory. The scientists used several techniques, such as ground penetrating radar, magnetometer surveys, and chemical soil analysis, as well as an instrument developed for field use which could detect the presence of chemicals associated with human decomposition. It was appropriately called the LABRADOR (Light-weight Analyzer for Buried Remains and Decomposition Odor Recognition). They combined the data and sent out the reports to direct law enforcement to the most likely spots to investigate.

It turned out that was the easy part. Along with Debra Tate, Sharon's sister, the group pushed for action over the next ten years, but further investigation got bogged down when some other dogs failed to alert in the same area, some digging produced no results, and—perhaps politics intervened—law enforcement lost interest, with the sheriff finally calling it quits and the US Park Service forbidding Paul to continue poking around. In the end, he said, "Who has the money to go to court and sue them? Eventually, you're done. They just laugh at you." He added, "But I know there are a bunch of murdered kids up there."

One of the forensic anthropologists, Dr. Arpad Vass, invited Buster and Paul on a special military missing-in-action expedition run by History Flight, a volunteer nonprofit that searches for MIA soldiers. The team traveled to the island of Tarawa in the South Pacific that had been the site of a terrible three-day battle in 1943 in which 1,200 Marines and 4,800 Japanese died. After search efforts were suspended in 1948, it was estimated that 335 American soldiers remained buried. The graves were plowed over to make an airstrip. On separate occasions, Buster and Dr. Vass surveyed the area, Buster using his nose and Dr. Vass collecting soil samples which he analyzed for human remains. Using a Geographic Information System, the project organizers overlaid the two sets of data onto aerial photos to determine the best places to dig. Their efforts resulted in the recovery of over 120 American Marines. Paul's investigatory work brought them to a trench where Buster alerted that turned out to contain 35 Marines, including missing Medal of Honor awardee Lt. Alexander Bonnyman, making it the first time in history a dog has found someone who had received the country's highest award for valor in action.

Buster and Paul's travels weren't over. In 2011, also for History Flight, they went to a small town in Belgium where an American Aircorp pilot, Robert Fenstermacher, had crashed in World War II, shot down by friendly fire in the fog of war. He had been MIA for 66 years. They located his remains which were shipped to the US, and he was finally buried in Arlington Cemetery. They also investigated in the Netherlands and the Ardennes Forest where the Battle of the Bulge took place. In honor of those who died, they walked the beach in Normandy, France. Paul was also able to visit the monument in Germany that listed his uncle killed in battle in WW II. Paul said, "When I was a kid, WW II was everything, movies, books, everything. Can you imagine what it was like for me to stand there on those actual locations?"

Matching a homicide detective with a human remains detection dog seems like common sense, but Paul said it wasn't done before Buster. In total, the team was credited with finding over 200 bodies through the course of their career together. Even after Buster lost a leg to cancer, he continued to work hard on murder cases all over the country. To follow his tracks is to unearth stories of serial killers, missing teenage girls and young boys, buried bodies, cold cases, and human depravity. You wouldn't know it from watching videos of Buster at work however. He was diligent, thorough, delighted when he made a discovery, and an all-around nice guy. He might not have been as eloquent as Paul who explained their role as "spokespersons for the victims," but his smile and wagging tail demonstrated his enthusiasm for his job.

In 2016, Buster and Paul were out playing in the yard at home in Benton when Buster suddenly keeled over. He died of a heart attack within minutes, breaking Paul's heart. Paul still misses Buster, but he is working with a new dog, Basco, who was born a week after Buster died. Paul summed up his life with Buster succinctly: "He changed my life in ways you can't even imagine."

LuLu, Dexter, and Gracie

DIANNE knows Golden Retrievers and she knows therapy work. She has had six Golden Retrievers, and she tries to go about seven days a month on her therapy rounds. "I love my dogs, and I love giving back," she said. She was already involved with Paws 4 Healing when she got LuLu. "I knew right away that she would be good as a therapy dog," she said. "You could see it from the kindness in her eyes." LuLu got certified at age three and loved going out. When DiAnne would tell her it was time for a bath, she would go hop in the shower. "She was a really fun dog to have around. I'm so grateful to her," said DiAnne. LuLu became an accomplished therapy dog after the early days when she once tried to grab a tennis ball off the leg of someone's walker. "They are Retrievers after all," said DiAnne.

She wasn't so sure about LuLu's male companion, Dexter, but took him on a trial visit to the Inyo Mono Association for the Handicapped. He put his head in the lap of a young adult with an expression that said, "Pet me." The two dogs formed a fabulous therapy team, visiting assisted-living facilities, care centers, and "challenged" classes in schools. They were hard at work when DiAnne acquired a beautiful four-month-old dark red Golden Retriever named Gracie. When Dexter and LuLu passed away, the therapy work fell to Gracie. DiAnne started training her, and she got certified at age two. Now six, she excels in the casual environments of the IMAH. "They file down to see her when we're hanging out in the lobby. They just love her," said DiAnne. Both Gracie and DiAnne find the therapy work very rewarding. "It makes me feel like I can help people who are less fortunate than myself," said DiAnne. "I am very fortunate. I live in a beautiful place. I love my work."

Therapy work is not without its challenges. The dogs are more hesitant in care centers with older people, especially in places with more of a hospital environment. "Dogs are very intuitive. It's amazing," said DiAnne. Sometimes handicapped children are afraid of the dogs at first because they have been very isolated, but they usually overcome that. "It's a good break for the kids, to have a dog to pet," DiAnne said. Once, when they opened the door of a care center, a resident with an ankle bracelet set off an alarm. "Gracie freaked," said DiAnne. She recognized that a visit wasn't in the cards, and she called it a day. "You have to know your dog and not push," she said. Another limitation is that the dogs need to be bathed before they can go visiting. "You don't want to be bathing your dog every week," DiAnne said. "It's not good for their skin."

Although Gracie knows when her vest goes on that she's going to work, she has many happy times accompanying DiAnne, to run errands or go horseback riding. "The truck is her home away from home," said DiAnne. She also takes Gracie on long walks off leash every day in the great walking areas around her house. "The Eastern Sierra is a good place to be a dog," she said.

Although DiAnne's husband had a Springer Spaniel when they met, he has changed his ways. "He's a Golden Retriever man now," she said. Knowing that they are going to outlive their dogs is hard. "We pray that we have them as long as we can," she said. "They are treasures on loan."

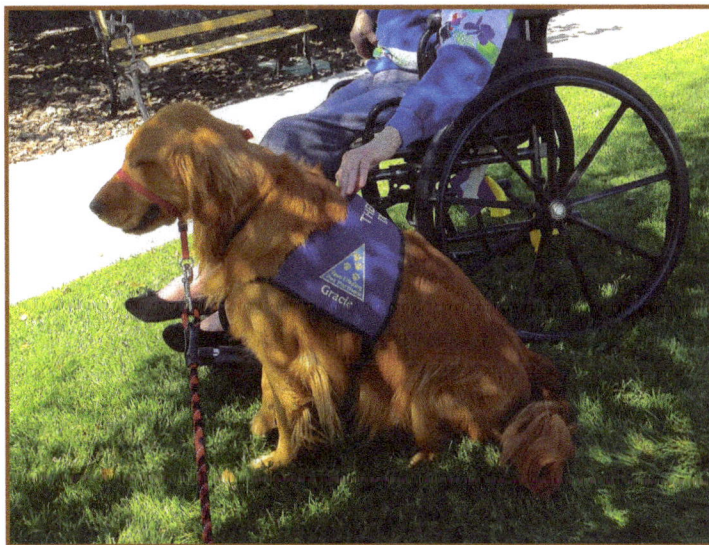

Tony and Roger

NINE-WEEK-OLD brothers, Tony and Roger, joined Patricia in the winter of 2016. The French Bulldog puppies quickly became familiar with an active lifestyle and settled in as her constant companions and shop dogs at the Red Lily florist shop in Mammoth Lakes.

"I wouldn't have gotten the breed if I couldn't pay enough attention to them," said Patricia. "Frenchies need a lot of attention. Sometimes people don't realize that and think they would make good apartment dogs. When they act up, it's sometimes because they were home alone. They're very needy."

As a florist, Patricia spends a lot of time in the back of the store, and Tony and Roger let her know when someone walks in. "It's quite useful," said Patricia. "It's weird when they're not here. People can just sneak in." Living up to the French Bulldog's reputation as a companion animal, they are very social. Roger especially loves the ladies. "Tony is more on his own agenda," said Patricia. "He's very busy at doing whatever Tony does."

Some customers come in specifically to visit with Tony and Roger, and there are lots of chuckles over the dogs' faces and antics. "They are hilarious," said Patricia. "They just have weird little personalities, very quirky. They're not like other dogs." Plus there are the noises they make, the grunts, squeaks, snuffles, and farts. "They sound like gremlins," said Patricia.

The two are big buddies with occasional sibling squabbles over bones and toys. Tony is serious when it comes to toys, obsessed with sticks and playing fetch. He picks out a special toy to focus on each day. "He is insistent. If you try to get him interested in another toy, it's a big 'no.' He goes back to the first one. Yesterday, it was a red squeaky toy. Today, it's a big white rope," said Patricia. He gets so possessive of a stick that he won't let go, even when she lifts him off the ground. "I have literally done bicep curls with him on the end of a stick," she said.

He also tries to take on any ball. They once encountered a large beach ball on a trail, and Tony attacked it and jumped on top. It slid under him, and he did a 360 in the air before landing on his feet and taking off after the ball. "I thought he was going to break his back," Patricia said.

He loves to swim, heartily throwing himself into lakes for a little recreation. That is not normal for a French Bulldog, but Tony didn't get that memo. Bigger and heavier, Roger does not share Tony's enthusiasm for water. When he was a puppy, he tried to chase some ducks and accidentally Supermanned into Bishop Pond. It has had a lasting effect. He does however like what comes out of the water. "He loves to eat raw trout. When he hears the 'zzzz' of the fishing line, he flips out because he knows there's a fish at the end of the line," Patricia said.

The two dogs embrace the Eastern Sierra lifestyle, going cross country skiing, camping, hiking, and playing in the snow. "They're very confident, sometimes overly so," said Patricia. "They have a real attitude."

Diller

THERE'S a reason they call him "Chill Dill." Here he is taking a break at the top of Diller Canyon two days after Lia got him from the shelter. "I hope this dog likes to ski," she told her ski partners as they navigated miles of rugged roads via 4×4, then on dirt bikes, and finally by foot hauling gear to the base of the giant mountain. It turned out that he did, big time, and that trip answered the question of what to call him. "He named himself," she said.

Diller was part of a big animal rescue where about 50 animals were confiscated from a ranch in Mariposa. Based on genetic testing and some guessing, he seems to be a blend of Malamute, White Shepherd, and Husky: maybe a White Malamute. Whatever he is, snow is in his DNA. "You see a lot more mountain dogs who look like him in Europe," said Lia who saw many look-a-likes while skiing Chamonix to Zermatt. She described a scene during a blizzard in the winter of 2018-19, when the wind was howling at 80 miles per hour, the snow was blowing sideways, and US Highway 395 was closed. She was surprised to see the dogs had gone outside in the storm and went to call them, peering into the darkness with her flashlight. There were Diller and the other dogs, lying in the snow, gnawing on some bones she had brought home from the meat market, happy as clams in the white swirling madness. "It was like some Arctic tundra scene," she said. "They were so happy out there with their bones. They're still wild in that way."

Summertime can be tough. If it gets hot, Lia has to put the dogs out on the porch at her June Lake house because their panting can keep her awake. Diller is generally more comfortable above the tree line. Lia and Diller went on an eight-day backpacking trip out of Rock Creek, on their own, with Diller packing his own food in a backpack. "I wouldn't do that on my own," said Lia. "It was really great to have a companion." They had a glorious time except the night there was a thunderstorm and it hailed. Diller normally preferred to sleep under the stars, but Lia had to force him into the tent that night because he is terrified of thunder and she was afraid he would just run.

They encountered another kind of thunder on that trip. As things developed, it turned out they would have to backtrack along a section of trail. Lia hates backtracking, so she came up with the idea to do it at night. They were walking along a creek about 9 p.m., heading back to Mono Pass, when they heard the sound of thundering hooves. It was a herd of pack animals, turned loose by their handlers, fired up, racing back to the station. Realization dawning on Lia, she tackled Dillon and threw herself and the dog off the trail, just as the charging animals pounded by. Left behind in the dust and ensuing silence, Lia and Dillon stared at each other. "He was fine, pretty relaxed, really," said Lia. "Like 'Oh, there goes a pack of wild horses.'"

Diller is unusually quiet. In the last six years, Lia has heard him bark only four or five times. "He's a silent observer," she said. He does get excited at the top of a ski run when it's time to head down. "He likes running," Lia said. He also enjoys taunting the other dogs to get them to chase him. In other ways, he doesn't resemble your average dog. He has no interest in tug-of-war or fetch. "I gave up with the Frisbee," said Lia. "It was like playing Frisbee with a cat."

At 80 pounds, with his fluffy fur, he can look intimidating, which comes in handy. As a biologist, Lia goes out on field projects into remote areas. She said, "One place had these sketchy squatters, people living illegally in some encampments. People were less likely to approach me with Diller. He definitely gave me extra assurance in that situation," she said. "And made my mom feel better."

With Diller as her partner, Lia has a love of connecting people to place through ecotourism and events through The Adventure Hub Eastern Sierra. Tales of their adventures can be heard on the adventure storytelling podcast, Boldly Went. From mountaineering to backpacking to protection, Diller has earned his keep. "You never know what you're going to get in a shelter dog," said Lia, "and we've ended up with this magical, majestic dog."

Rudi

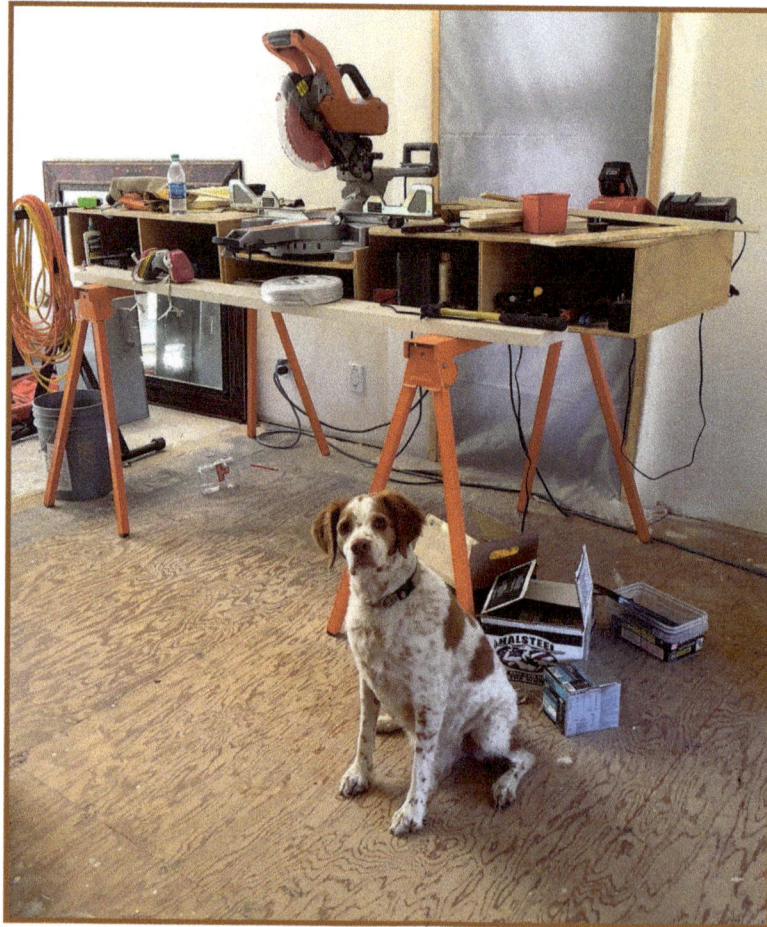

"**WE** joke that we rescued him from the trunk of a car," Deborah said. She and her husband, Rod, had arranged to meet the breeder in Bakersfield at a spot halfway between their houses. The breeder arrived first and let the litter of American Brittany puppies roam safely in the trunk while they waited. Deborah and Rod selected Rudi and drove away with him, completing the rescue.

Brittanys are an old hunting breed developed in the Brittany province of France. Deborah and Rod are not hunters, but they wanted an easy, medium-sized dog to travel with them for camping, hiking, biking, and kayaking. Brittanys are sometimes referred to as a spaniel although their working characteristics are more like those of a pointer. Some breeders draw a distinction between American and French Brittanys, the American dogs being larger and having more of a running style.

Deborah and Rod found out about the running part. When they lived on a large ranch in Crowley Lake, Rudi had plenty of room to race around chasing everything and satisfy his need for exercise. After they moved to a smaller property in Bishop, Rudi's need for stimulation became apparent. Rod began taking him to his job site where there is more action. Over time, his mellow and affectionate nature has endeared him to the crew, and they are happy to welcome him every day, as well as threaten to secretly take him home with them. "It started as a benefit to him," said Deborah, "but it grew into this mutual benefit thing." Rudi brings a good vibe to the site, lowering stress and brightening the workers' day, not an easy task. "Plus he can make the rounds at lunchtime," Rod chuckled.

Rudi's parents were bird dogs, and Rudi instinctually goes into a point position to indicate a squirrel or bird to Rod, in case he suddenly takes up hunting. Rod said, "He can hold that position for an hour, without moving a muscle, until you call him off. If the squirrel jumps to another tree, Rudi will go point under that tree. He's very patient." Rudi isn't particularly interested in large animals, even other dogs. In Mammoth Lakes, a young deer once approached him to play, but Rudi ignored him and went to find some birds. Another day, Rod took Rudi on a service call, and Rudi spotted a small black object standing out in the grass. He immediately began pointing and stood stock still until Rod showed him that it was a landscape light fixture.

Rudi is very people-oriented, greeting everyone at the job site when he arrives in the morning. Deborah said he demonstrates similar behaviors when they visit dog parks, even if he doesn't know anyone there. "He will literally go to each human, kind of greet them, and sit there with them like he's their dog," she said. "Then he goes to the next person." Rudi thinks it's his job to hang out with people.

His devotion to his own people proved very important in protecting the ducks that frequent the ponds on Deborah and Rod's property. When they moved to the new house, they would reprimand Rudi if they saw he was starting to fixate on the ducks. It's not an easy thing for a bird dog to coexist with resident ducks, but Rudi showed how much he wants to please his people. "He really listens to us," said Deborah. "He's a good dog. We feel very lucky."

Whoopi

SOON after Whoopi came into Barbi's life, she knew she would have to do something with such an exceptional dog. "She was a once-in-a-lifetime dog," she said. Whoopi was smart, way smart, and loved to wow everyone with a new trick. If you sneezed, she'd bring the kleenex box. If you said you were thirsty, she would bring you a water bottle. Barbi started looking around for an outlet for the dog's sensitivity to people. Therapy dogs were not really a thing back then, but she did find an organization in Los Angeles.

Whoopi and Barbi set to work, and Whoopi was certified at age two, passing her test with flying colors and making her proud owner burst into tears. She and Barbi began working at the Veterans

Administration in Westwood, at the Foundation for the Junior Blind, at the McBride School in Culver City, and all around Los Angeles. They did a lot of work with the VA because the veterans really appreciated the big black Lab with the sparkling personality.

As the years went by, Barbi joined the board of the therapy dog organization, and when she and Whoopi were in Mammoth Lakes, they continued volunteering for therapy work, especially enjoying cheering up the folks at a local association for the handicapped. When it developed that the administrator of the therapy dog organization was pulling some shenanigans with the charity's funds, Barbi and the other board members resigned en masse, collapsing the organization. Now what? The board re-grouped and decided to start their own chapters in their respective communities. Flash forward many years, Paws 4 Healing has ten chapters throughout Southern California and is affiliated with Pet Partners, a national association.

Therapy dogs can be certified at two levels: predictable and complex. Predictable dogs are those that are good with people but have some restrictions, for example, if they don't like kids or are too small to be safe around them. Complex dogs have to pass a tougher exam, but then can go into any institution. The Eastern Sierra Paws 4 Healing chapter has about 12 big dogs who have all passed their complex certification.

Barbi knew that Whoopi's work benefited people, but she had one opportunity to quantify the effect. Mammoth Hospital had called and asked them to come in. An eight-year-old girl was in the intensive care unit, suffering from pneumonia. The girl could barely breathe and was beside herself with fear, her blood pressure and heart rate sky high. Tension in the room was thick when Whoopi and Barbi arrived. The parents, nurses, and the doctor were silent and nervous. Barbi had brought a rug to put on the bed if the little girl wanted the dog to join her. She said she did. "Paws up," said Barbi. Whoopi put her paws on the edge of the bed, and Barbi hoisted her up. To her astonishment, as soon as the girl put her arms around the dog, the monitors went straight down, as her heart rate and blood pressure returned normal. "That proved it," said Barbi.

On another occasion, they were again called in to Mammoth Hospital to meet with an injured girl. The little girl's brother had thrown a food container at her, resulting in a deep cut that required stitches. The girl was panicked, screaming and refusing to cooperate. Barbi began calmly talking to the girl, pointing out that if she agreed to the stitches, she would have an awesome photo for Show and Tell at school, with Whoopi, the stitches, and the missile. The girl wanted that photo with Whoopi, and the stitching was accomplished.

Although Whoopi now lives only in our memories, her legacy endures in the local therapy dogs and in the minds of the many people she helped. Barbi said, "She changed people's lives."

81

Photo Credits

Photographs were reproduced with the permission of the copyright holder. Photographers are listed below.

Page	Photographer	Page	Photographer
pg. 0-3	Coryl McGrath	pg. 38, 40, 41	Leo Hertz
pg. 4	Alix Ginter	pg. 42	Daniel Hansen
pg. 6, 8	Anne Parkes	pg. 44	Devin Perry
pg. 10	Lea Belgarde	pg. 46	Nina Sage
pg. 12	Ryan Salay	pg. 48, 50, 51	Christi Contois
pg. 12, 14, 15	Christina Ackerman	pg. 52, 54	Eric Johnson
pg. 16, 18, 19	Jennifer Roeser	pg. 56, 59	Nick Souza Photography
pg. 20	Sonja Bush	pg. 60	Pam Barker
pg. 22	Matt Uhry	pg. 62, 64, 65	Blair Hunewill
pg. 24	Mike De Lannoy	pg. 66, 69	Paul Dostie
pg. 26	Jennifer K. Crittenden	pg. 70, 71	DiAnne Brown
pg. 28	Doug Johnson	pg. 72	Patricia Vander
pg. 30	Joe Echenique	pg. 74, 76, 77	Lia Webb
pg. 32	Patti Echenique	pg. 78	Deborah Paulson
pg. 34, 37	Nick Souza Photography	pg. 80	Bonnie Colgan

COVER:

Background: Leslie Wells

Top (l-r): Patti Echenique, Nick Souza Photography, Blair Hunewill, Ryan Salay, Lea Belgarde
Bottom (l-r): Matt Uhry, Anne Parkes, Daniel Hansen, DiAnne Brown, Mike De Lannoy

Acknowledgments

THIS was the funnest book project ever. Here's to the dogs, our hard-working Eastern Sierra dogs who herd and retrieve, who find and comfort, who work without complaint in snow, dirt, and ashes, as well as our pets who become part of our families. My sincere appreciation goes out to the dogs' humans, who shared their stories, their memories, and sometimes their tears. Thank you to those who edited, clarified, explained, pored through photos, and put up with my many questions. I learned an incredible amount during the process and am grateful for your patience. Thank you to my parents, Kathie and Ray, for digging up a photo of Jet and re-telling the stories of her exploits. My love as always goes to the Harvey boys, Luc, Julian, and Tom, who support and encourage me in small ways and large, and were always willing to look at more cute dog pictures.

A Word about Shelters

MANY of the dogs in this book are purebred, acquired from commercial breeders. You may be asking, where are the shelter dogs? Don't you care about the rescues? A few of the dogs were rescue dogs, but most serious working dogs are bred for a particular purpose. Which reminds me of a recent New Yorker cartoon: Two dogs are watching a man work at his computer. One dog says to the other, "They were bred to stare."

Several of the humans included in this book devote significant effort to our local shelters, volunteering and donating funds. Some were involved with establishing and operating Eastern Sierra Dog Rescue in Bishop, the Whitmore Animal Shelter, and ICARE, an Inyo-Mono nonprofit dedicated to the welfare of companion animals. Their achievements have resulted in greatly reduced euthanasia rates at our local shelters. Your donations to care for our homeless canines would also be much appreciated.

Nonprofits

A portion of the proceeds from sales of this book will be donated to Eastside K-9, Paws 4 Healing, Guide Dogs for the Blind, Eastern Sierra Agility Group, and Mono County Sheriff Search and Rescue Team. They would also welcome your contributions to continue their work.

Index

www.ingramcontent.com/pod-product-compliance
Lightning Source LLC
Chambersburg PA
CBHW061415090426
42742CB00026B/3476

* 9 7 8 1 9 5 0 8 3 5 0 0 3 *